From The Desk Of
Judy Doll

Religious
Ethics
and
Pastoral Care

THEOLOGY AND PASTORAL CARE SERIES
edited by
Don S. Browning

Faith Development and Pastoral Care
by James W. Fowler

The Family and Pastoral Care
by Herbert Anderson

Religious Ethics and Pastoral Care
by Don S. Browning

Ritual and Pastoral Care
by Elaine Ramshaw

DON S. BROWNING

Religious Ethics and Pastoral Care

Don S. Browning, *editor*

THEOLOGY AND PASTORAL CARE

FORTRESS PRESS
PHILADELPHIA

Library of Congress Cataloging in Publication Data

Browning, Don S.
   Religious ethics and pastoral care.

   (Theology and pastoral care series)
   Bibliography: p.
   1. Pastoral theology. 2. Pastoral counseling.
  3. Religious ethics. I. Title. II. Series.
   BV4011.5.B77 1983   241'.641   83-5589
   ISBN 0-8006-1725-8

Printed in the United States of America 1-1725
94 93 92 91 90   2 3 4 5 6 7 8 9 10

To my partners in ethical dialogue
Chris Gamwell
James Gustafson
Robin Lovin

Contents

Series Foreword

Our purpose in the Theology and Pastoral Care Series is to present ministers and church leaders with a series of readable books that will (1) retrieve the theological and ethical foundations of the Judeo-Christian tradition for pastoral care, (2) develop lines of communication between pastoral theology and the other disciplines of theology, (3) create an ecumenical dialogue on pastoral care, and (4) do this in such a way as to affirm yet go beyond the recent preoccupation of pastoral care with secular psychotherapy and the other social sciences.

The books in this series are written by authors who are well acquainted with psychology, psychotherapy, and the other social sciences. All of the authors affirm the importance of these disciplines for modern societies and for ministry in particular, but they see them also as potentially destructive of human values unless they are guided in their practical application by tested religious and ethical traditions. But to retrieve the best of the Judeo-Christian tradition for the church's care and counseling is a challenging intellectual task—a task to which few writers in the area of pastoral care have attended with sufficient thoroughness. This series addresses that task out of a broad ecumenical stance, with all of the authors taking an ecumenical approach to theology. Besides a vigorous investigation of Protestant resources, there are specific treatments of pastoral care in Judaism and Catholicism.

We hope that the series will help ministers and church leaders view afresh the theological and ethical foundations of care and counseling. All of the books have a practical dimension, but even more important than that, they help us see care and counseling differently. Compared with writings of the last thirty years in this field, some of the books will seem startlingly different. They will need to be read and pondered with care. But I have little doubt that the series will make a profound and lasting impact upon the way we understand and practice our care for one another.

In *Religious Ethics and Pastoral Care* I continue an argument begun in *The Moral Context of Pastoral Care,* namely, that before we can exercise care (or even know what it is) we have to have a religious ethic. In some instances we can use our inherited religio-ethical traditions without reconstructing them; in other instances we have to reconstruct them, or at least certain aspects of them. The minister doing pastoral care must be an ethical thinker and understand the methods of ethical thinking. In every act of care, the minister must also be able to relate judgments about how people *should live* with judgments about where people *actually are.* And finally, the minister should have both the skills and the judgment to help people gradually move through the long journey of closing the gap between that ethical ideal and reality. What this might mean and how it might happen is what this book is about.

The practical payoff of the book is largely in the last couple of chapters. For those who cannot wait, these can be read after the case studies in chapter 7 have been finished. But the argument of the book—and the logic of the title—in many ways requires that it be read from beginning to end. Chapters 5 and 6 put forth a method for practical moral thinking that may help us reestablish the moral contexts of our care when these contexts seem unstable or about to collapse. Frequently we can enjoy the luxury of relying on the wisdom of our inherited moral traditions, but when these traditions come unglued we sometimes have to resort to the kind of moral reflection I am proposing in this book in order to orient ourselves to our care for one another.

CHAPTER 1

Pluralism, Modernity, and Care

After the experience of the last several decades most of us are willing to admit that modern societies, and the forces which produce them, are ambiguous. Some things about modern societies—"modernity" as the sociologists call it—are good, but there are other things about which we have doubts. Life in the context of modernity entails real gains and real losses. Few of us are willing to give up the increased abundance, the new conveniences, the additional freedom, and the increasingly specialized approach to our problems that characterize modern societies. But most of us at times are afflicted with nostalgia for the simpler, more organic, less rationalized, and perhaps less lonely lives that sociologists say existed in medieval and primitive societies.

The losses that come with modernity are many, and the gains are many too. I want to focus attention on a particular kind of gain and loss that affects the way we treat one another, especially in times of personal confusion, anguish, and incapacity.

DIFFERENTIATED HELP

In modern societies our disciplines of care and counseling have become increasingly specialized and separated from one another. By disciplines of care I mean those institutionalized traditions—such as religion, psychology, and medicine—that try to help people who are experiencing spiritual, mental, or physical problems. In modern societies these disciplines become, as the social scientists put it, "differentiated." In primitive societies, these several traditions or areas of life were more or less indistinct. In fact, religion was the organizing canopy addressing the entire field of human difficulties, and psychological and physical problems were seen to be, partially or wholly, religio-ethical in nature.[1] But in modern societies the spiritual, psychological, and physical dimensions of life have become broken apart, both institutionally and conceptually. Our churches and synagogues, our psychological professions, and our medical professions and hospitals are all relatively autonomous as institutions. They also tend to have separate bodies of theory and practice. It is true that they sometimes cooperate and in some ways interpenetrate each other's spheres of special focus. But this is the point: from positions of relative autonomy they frequently feel the need to discover practical and theoretical ways of *relating* to one another. The problem of modernity in every area of life, and in the areas of care and counseling as well, is how to create an integrated world out of the fragmented parts.

The gains connected with such loss are ambiguous. For instance, in helping a person it is sometimes useful to differentiate psychological, physical, and religio-ethical problems from one another. Benjamin, age five, was in a car accident while visiting his uncle's home in another town. For several months following the accident Benjamin was afraid to leave his parents; he was especially apprehensive about riding in other people's cars. His apprehension is not physiologically grounded; neither is it the result of some difficulty in his parents' religio-ethical world view. His problem is simply due to an accident that traumatized him and left him very frightened. On the other hand, Benjamin may handle his accident-induced separation anxiety better if his doctor gives him some medication to relieve the muscle strain in his neck. And his parents' religious faith may help him feel an extra "presence" needed to give him security the next time he is temporarily apart from them. In Benjamin's case it is appropriate to separate the various perspectives for purposes of diagnosis, but it is also necessary to relate them once again when it comes time to help. If the lines of differentiation between the disciplines are hardened and dogmatically fixed, however, and we bring neither religion nor medicine back into the picture, our temporary gain may turn quickly into a sad, and possibly tragic, loss.

CARING IN THE
PLURALISTIC SITUATION

Our purpose in what follows is to help relate once again two of these perspectives—the religio-ethical and the psychological. This book is addressed primarily to ministers and other religious leaders whose responsibility it is to construct a religio-ethical universe of meaning while at the same time helping people with various problems in living. In addressing these religious leaders we hope to maintain a special awareness of the pluralistic situation in which they function. Every minister in our society, every lay leader, every religiously engaged person works and acts in a pluralistic cultural and social situation. This means that they function in a society marked by a plethora of different religious, cultural, and moral views. In a pluralistic society assumptions about these basic matters are not always widely shared. In addition this pluralistic situation affects our assumptions about how we help people—assumptions about what the people need, what their problems really are, who has a right to help them, what the goals of that helping should be, and which values if any should control the helping process.

The Question

The question I am asking can be stated in several ways, all of which are interrelated. Let me state it first in its most parochial form: Is it possible to do pastoral care in a pluralistic age? Phrasing the question this way suggests that I am not interested solely in what pastors do to care for or counsel with the members of their own congregations. I am also interested in what pastors do to help people outside the church. How does the minister ground and articulate her philosophy of care on the board of the local mental health service upon which she sits, or on the public school committee of which she is a member, or at the local psychiatric clinic where she is a part-time chaplain, or in assessing the human services policy of her mayor or governor? In short, how do the minister's religio-ethical convictions inform issues of care and counseling both within her own congregation and among the larger public world which is also an arena for her ministry?

In modern societies the public world is invariably a pluralistic world. Gone is the day when everyone in a particular community is a Christian, even a nominal Christian. Gone is the day when pluralism meant nothing more than facing some of the doctrinal differences between Baptists, Methodists, and Presbyterians. The public world is increasingly made up of individuals and groups of diverse faiths, different moral commitments, and conflicting life styles. This is the way the public world is outside the church—and increasingly, we must admit, inside the church as well.

More and more, particular congregations are public groups of people with enormous differences in their religious, ethical, and life-style commitments, or lack of them. The consensus existing in many churches and parishes today is, literally, constructed. With an eye toward her religious tradition on the one hand and the needs of her people on the other, the minister uses her leadership again and again to construct and reconstruct a workable identity that is more or less shared by most of her people. This pluralism makes consensus, both inside and outside the church, increasingly difficult to achieve. It affects the big issues, of course—such as our basic beliefs and moral convictions—but it also affects and complicates the way we care for and counsel one another.

Church and World

Most books on care and counseling written during the last thirty years, whether religious or secular, say little to acknowledge this pluralistic situation. Books on pastoral care are generally written in a parochial spirit; they are addressed to ministers working with people within their own parishes. It is generally assumed that the members of a given church live in a relatively homogenous religious and moral world. These parishioners may not believe or abide by this religio-ethical world as intensely as they should, but the books are written as though most everyone the pastor works with knows what this world is. Hence, these books, for the most part, emphasize the process or technique, the how-to-do-it character of care and counseling rather than the substantive goals. Pluralism exists both inside and outside the church, but in neither place is it being handled very well in our care and counseling. Think of the following situations within the church:

In a small Presbyterian church in the suburbs of a southern city a young man and woman start attending church. Word soon gets around that the couple are living together but are not married. Some members of the congregation don't seem to care but others are outraged. People on both sides of the argument consider themselves good church members, good Christians. Both sides appeal to the love of God—some in order to defend the sanctity of marriage, others in order to justify tolerance and looking the other way.

The minister of a middle-class church is on the board of the community medical center. She votes for the center to distribute contraceptive information, without parental consent, to sexually active teenagers. Parents later complain when it is learned that several girls from the church's youth group are on the pill, including the minister's own daughter. What does she do? How does she handle the conflict, both public and parochial, that develops?

An upper-middle-class Methodist church in a Chicago suburb wakes up to the high percentage of teenage suicides in its community. Pressures and expectations on the part of the parents—and indeed of the entire community—are suspected as being major contributing factors. The values of the people, their whole style of life, may indeed be the culprit. But how should the issue be defined and how should the church proceed?

The teenagers of an inner-city Hispanic community are organizing into gangs. Should the minister and the congregation cooperate with the police in breaking up the gangs, or should they support the gangs, leaving them intact, and subtly try to redirect gang energies—even though it may mean ignoring some of the gang lawlessness? The congregation is in conflict about how to proceed.

All of these examples point to profound issues in care. None of these issues can be handled by the private ministrations of the minister alone or of a few lay leaders. All of them involve conflict and controversy within the church. Addressing the issues will entail clarifying the fundamental self-definitions and policies of the church as these apply both to its own inner life and to its stance in and mission to the world, that is, to the diverse publics outside its boundaries.

THE NEED FOR
PRACTICAL MORAL THINKING

Care is a complex practical activity. Like any practical action, it is composed of several levels of reasoning and decision. Care as a practical action does not appear to be complex when we simply follow the dictates of the caring traditions handed down to us by our culture from generation to generation. But when modernity, institutional differentiation, and pluralism set in, our traditions of care become confused and diverse—like most other aspects of society. As Peter Berger would put it, the "plausibility structures" of society begin to crumble, including those which sanction our practices of care.[2] When these legitimating structures begin to collapse, we can no longer unreflectively rely on the received tradition to guide our practical activity. We have to start thinking. We have to go back to the beginning and go through all the complexities of fresh practical thinking. This does not mean that we can disregard tradition. But under the pressure of conflict and crisis we begin thinking about the tradition critically. By critical, of course, I do not mean something negative and destructive. Rather, I mean simply a reflective process of examination, analysis, and testing. When we participate in this process we learn just how complex fresh practical thinking really is.

It is the basic thesis of this book that for congregations to reconstitute their caring practices, they must become adept in the skills of practical thinking. Such critical practical thinking is inevitably moral thinking; in fact it is a practical moral rationality of a particular kind. Because of the inevitable relation which I believe exists between religion and morality, this practical moral rationality is actually, at depth, a practical religious ethic. Hence, my argument is that our traditions of care, both within and outside the church, need to be reconstituted under the guidance of a critical practical moral theology (as Catholics would call it), or theological ethics (as Protestants would call it), or religious ethics (as philosophers would call it). (I will use these terms more or less interchangeably, only gradually introducing distinctions among them.) Under the pressures of pluralism the very goals of our care often come under question. To reconstitute these goals our care must once again be guided by a normative discipline—by a critical and practical religious ethics or moral theology.

For several decades the mainline Christian churches, both Protestant and Catholic, have been tempted increasingly to handle questions of care and counseling without the guidance of normative theological disciplines. This is due partly to the relativizing pressures of our pluralistic society and partly to the influence that the secular disciplines of psychiatry and psychology have had on the care and counseling practices of ministers and priests. But whatever the reasons, for years now we have been trying to address problems in marriage, sexuality, child rearing, work, adulthood, aging, and death on more or less technical psychological grounds and without the benefit of articulated normative views of these areas of human life. Our pluralistic moral and cultural situation and the need for a critical practical moral theology of care clearly go hand in hand. Or to put it more simply: our confusions must be met with articulate and practical theological thinking.

But it is not just the care of churches that is confronted by the strains of pluralism and modernity. The care and counseling of our secular institutions of psychiatry, psychology, and social work are afflicted with similar challenges and confusions. Take the examples mentioned above. It is not just the church that is reevaluating the institution of marriage. Governments formulating policy in the area of welfare allowances, tax deductions, and inheritance laws are also struggling with similar concerns. The problem of the minister whose young people were sexually active was first of all a policy issue for a tax-supported community medical facility. The church confronting the issue of teenage suicide was facing what in the first instance was a community-wide problem. The teenage gangs forming in the inner city were disturbing and threatening the entire community, not just the church. Their existence was a public problem, not just a parochial one. And the response of the local church must be defended before the entire community in a public way with reasons that, although grounded in faith, can at the same time be made understandable to the diverse publics affected by the gang activities.

Pastoral care in a pluralistic age must be guided by a critically and philosophically oriented practical moral theology or theological ethics. This will be necessary for handling issues of care for the diverse publics within specific churches, and it will be necessary for addressing the issues of care for the diversity found in the public world outside the church.

CHAPTER 2

The Estrangement
of
Care from Ethics

PRACTICAL MORAL THINKING

It is the thesis of this book that care and counseling must once again become related to and grounded in ethics. This is true not only for pastoral care but for secular care as well. For pastoral care this means relating the church's care and counseling once again to practical moral theology or religious ethics. For the more secular traditions of care, counseling, and psychotherapy, it means relating once again to moral philosophy, which itself always has a religious dimension.

But this thesis involves three subsidiary points.

Critical

If it is to guide care in a pluralistic society, this practical religious ethics or moral theology must in the first place be critical and philosophical. In case the use of such words as "critical" and "philosophical" in this context jars the sensibilities of some of my clergy readers, let me say this: by using these words I do not mean to deny the confessional origins of all religious thinking—indeed of all thinking whatsoever—but I do mean to assert that in our time theology in general and practical theology in particular must be willing to reflect critically on itself and advance reasons for its actions that will be intelligible to those who do not share its faith. Such critical reflection and accounting means using something like a "revised correlational method" for doing practical theology, a concept to which I will return in chapter 5.

Related to Dynamic Psychology

Second, even where pastoral care is grounded in practical moral theology, it must not lose contact with dynamic psychology. By dynamic psychology I mean those depth-psychological traditions associated with the names of Freud, Jung, Carl R. Rogers, Harry S. Sullivan, Erik Erikson, Fritz Perls, Eric Berne, and—more recently—Heinz Kohut and the British school of object relations. It is these traditions which have taught us to be sensitive to the origins of human behavior—its childhood beginnings, its unconscious substrata, its schedules of development, and its motivations and needs. One of the interests of this book, and one of the major intellectual agendas of our time, is to bring ethics and dynamic psychology back into closer relation. Ethics is needed to guide dynamic psychology, but dynamic psychology is needed to overcome the moralism into which ethics, religious or secular, can so easily fall.

System-Oriented

Third, pastoral care is primarily the care of systems and secondarily the care of individuals within these systems. This is a point well made by E. Mansell Pattison[1] and, before that, by Robert Bonthius.[2] It is certainly a theme in my earlier *The Moral Context of Pastoral Care*.[3] Pattison, however, states the issue most commendably in his *Pastor and Parish—A Systems Approach*. From Pattison's viewpoint, care of systems is central because individual identity and individual behavior are both largely shaped by the identity and action patterns of the institutional systems of which persons are a part. But Pattison tends to overemphasize the technical and sociological aspects of his systems theory. He does not fully acknowledge the truth that the forming of systems is a moral enterprise and that to shape institutions in a pluralistic society requires a method of critical moral rationality—a method which inevitably has religious dimensions.

THE CASE OF JIM AND
BETTY FARR

I will illustrate and develop these points by presenting here a pastoral case and making extended commentary on it. The case is offered not in order to model ways of counseling people in pastoral settings, but in order to help us modify our picture of pastoral care and become sensitized to the issues often ignored in the standard case studies usually provided in most literature on pastoral care.

The case in question emerged during a seminar for ministers and advanced theological students. Each participant was invited to present the case of an actual pastoral care episode. That done, they were asked to provide extended theological-ethical and psychological commentaries on the case. It was hoped that by this procedure we might begin actually to sketch a practical theology of care, one that would contain a vital dynamic-psychological component.

The case of Jim and Betty Farr, as we shall call them, involved a situation of marital strain and tension. As they brought their problem to their minister, it appeared on the surface to center around Betty's problem with alcohol. The couple, in their early forties, had two teenage children. She had come from a vaguely Catholic background. He was from German stock, with an equally loose relation to the Lutheran tradition. At the time, the Farrs were occasionally attending a local Lutheran church. They had met in California where both had gone as young adults in order to escape what each perceived as a rather dreary life at home. They had met while Jim was working on a Ph.D. in chemistry. Betty had helped put her husband through school.

By way of preparation for the psychological interpretation to follow, the seminar received the following information concerning the developmental backgrounds of the Farrs. Mrs. Farr was one of several children. Her childhood memories centered around her mother's constant criticism of her and coldness toward her. This criticism seemed always to have existed and to have been aimed more at Betty than at the other children. When Betty was an early teenager her mother became ill and eventually died. Betty began at that point to play a new and much more responsible role in the family. Her siblings began to depend on her, and her father praised her lavishly for her newfound dependability.

Mr. Farr's early memories centered around a significant family trauma that occurred when he was about six years old. His father, who had been a rather dashing and successful businessman, suddenly lost everything in the Great Depression. Jim's father and mother both reacted to the attendant social demotion with depression and increasing detachment. Jim remembers his mother becoming sick shortly thereafter and remaining sick until her rather early death. Both Jim and Betty seemed old for their years, constricted in affect, and generally depressed.

The minister, whom we shall call Peter Spicer, was a more-than-middle-aged pastor. As he developed the case for members of the seminar, he came across as deeply imbued with his rich Lutheran liturgical tradition. But in spite of these marks of ecclesiastical self-consciousness, he had for some years also been involved with psychology and counseling and saw these as important aspects of his ministry. Indeed, it was interesting to note that Pastor Spicer—and for that matter all the seminar participants—found it easier to develop a psychological interpretation of the Farrs than to interpret the case from a theological-ethical point of view.

A Psychological Interpretation

Pastor Spicer developed his interpretation from a basically psychoanalytic point of view, one strongly influenced, however, by the more recent developments in psychoanalytic theory associated with the late Chicago psychoanalyst Heinz Kohut.[4] Kohut, Pastor Spicer explained, accepted most of the classic psychoanalytic theories but supplemented them by introducing a theory of the self. Freud's later structural theory had divided the personality into the well-known ego, superego, and id. Kohut added to this famous tripartite division a theory of the self. Building on the work of Heinz Hartman, Kohut defined the self as an affect-laden representation (image, picture) of our being and functioning. It is distinguishable from the ego, which is the personality's center of initiative, control, and protection. The ego, as Freud spoke of it, did not include the idea of a representation or image (self-image) of its own initiative, control, and other activities.

The minister felt that both Mr. and Mrs. Farr had defects in their self-representations and had built their marriage on a precarious system of exchanges designed to support and maintain their fragile sense of self-cohesion. From one perspective Pastor Spicer thought, and the seminar concurred, that Mrs. Farr could be seen to have developed an oedipal relation with her father. Yet Pastor Spicer believed that there might be something earlier and deeper that needed to be considered. The oedipal conflict usually comes at around the age of five or six, when the child has developed suffi-ciently to be aware of the sexual differentiation between his parents. But Betty's basic difficulty was possibly preoedipal (what analysts call prestructural because it is prior to the differentiation of the psycho-logical structure of ego, id, and superego that occurs at the resolu-tion of the oedipal conflict). Betty's relation to her cold and rejecting mother, thought Spicer, had dealt an enduring blow to her narcissis-tic investment in her own self-image, robbing her of her primitive yet essential sense of self-regard and self-appreciation. Because of

Betty's buried resentment toward her mother, some guilt doubtlessly developed at the time of her mother's death. But what was probably more important dynamically was the new role that Betty began to play in the home following her mother's death, and the appreciation that her father gave her for it. His response doubtlessly served to compensate and meet some of Betty's own unsatisfied "narcissistic" (affect-laden self-regard) needs.

Mr. Farr's main personality deficiencies were also seen by Pastor Spicer as rather deep and preoedipal. They centered around a wound, also narcissistic in character, to another aspect of the early sense of self—what Kohut has called the "idealized self." By the idealized self, Spicer explained, Kohut had in mind the ways in which very young children develop a sense of a warm, appreciated, and cohesive self by identifying with other strong and competent people, generally parents, in their environment.[5] The blow to Jim Farr's idealized self came when his father suffered a business reversal that threw both himself and the entire family into a traumatic and deeply felt loss of prestige. This loss was defeating to the young boy because it occurred at the time of his first attempts to form a sense of selfhood around his identification with his father. Young Jim, along with his father and mother, retreated into a mode of detachment. His preoccupation with money and the trappings of success, which was all too evident, was his way, Spicer believed, of compensating for his early depletion in "narcissistic supplies."

Hence, the Farrs needed each other, but not for viable or enduring reasons. Betty needed to have someone to help, to serve, and to enhance. She hoped in return to receive a great deal of appreciation that would compensate for the old lack of self-regard and self-cohesion. In the early days of the marriage, when she was working so hard to help her husband educate and establish himself, she seemed to get this return from their relationship. Once established, however, Jim's withdrawn and vulnerable self could not easily continue to deliver what his wife so desperately needed. Betty's deepened needs for a confirming and admiring presence, aggravated by her recent problems with alcohol, were met by Jim with even more profound remoteness. Yet his own sense of selfhood, although highly vulnerable, appeared more stable; after all, his apparent vocational and monetary success propped up his own fragile sense of idealized self-worth. But Jim was agitated by Betty's needs and she was desperate over his lack of responsiveness.

A Theological-Ethical
Interpretation

Pastor Spicer's theological-ethical analysis of the case was much briefer and less complex. He had clearly put the weight of his intellectual energy into his psychological interpretation. He made no effort to assess from a theological perspective where the Farrs were in their lives and in their moral and religious development. His theological-ethical interpretation centered on the importance of offering, on the part of both him and his congregation, a warm and supportive relation to the couple. Through that relation, he hoped to show forth the love of God for each of them. Such a relation, he thought, would address with considerable accuracy the narcissistic wounds that both of them suffered. It would provide a consistent sense of affirmation or "mirroring" that would support Mrs. Farr's deep need for a fundamental level of appreciation. And a similar steadfast and consistent relation with Mr. Farr would help build his basic sense of self and enable him better to withstand the inevitable threats to his self-esteem that would come when the ephemeral values of economic and vocational success began to fade. Pastor Spicer made reference to 1 Cor. 13:12–13, a biblical recognition of our need to perceive a confirming face and to be deeply understood by both our neighbor and our God: "For now we see in a mirror dimly, but then *face to face*. Now I know in part; then I shall understand fully, *even as I have been fully understood.*"

On the other hand, Pastor Spicer felt that saving the marriage "was not the important thing." He said nothing in his interpretation about a theology or ethics of marriage, sexuality, or interpersonal relations. In fact, he said nothing about what marriage is supposed to be, and in that light how the Farrs' marriage could be seen from a theological-ethical perspective as problematic.

What Pastor Spicer did say was that the growth of Jim and Betty as individuals was the proper goal to pursue. Their individual growth would in the long run best serve the couple and their family. But he did not define theologically what he meant by growth, or indicate why their growth as individuals should be the primary value controlling the goals of pastoral work.

Pastor Spicer's final recommendation to Jim and Betty ran as follows: "I hope that during the next month you can remain in close contact with the church and with me. I want you to experience the love we share in this church, and for that love to sink in and become a part of your own deepest selves. But some of your difficulties go back a long way in your lives. It will be best if you see a professional counselor who has the time and skill to look at some of the old wounds that are apparently still festering and infecting your present relationship to each other."

Pastor Spicer believed that his own pastoral care and the care of his church should in this instance be supportive of a more specialized work that would permit real "transference" to develop along lines not likely to occur in the less-structured general relationships of the church. In addition, for a more direct approach to control of her symptoms, he felt that Mrs. Farr should go to Alcoholics Anonymous. In fact, Pastor Spicer was pleased to announce that she had been willing to do so.

Reflections on the Pastoral Interpretation

Peter Spicer's theological-ethical analysis was more revealing for what it left unsaid than for the position actually espoused. His style of theological interpretation illustrates a widespread tendency for ministers and professional theologians to do practical theological interpretations on the basis of a few high-level religious metaphors—such as the love of God or the goodness of creation—which they interpret quite abstractly and then apply to a whole range of concrete situations, ignoring in the process a number of necessary intervening judgments. At one level, Pastor Spicer's position must be correct: consistency of recognition—enduring love both human and divine—precisely mediated is surely what both the Christian faith and the dynamics of Jim and Betty's personal needs require. But having said that, much more remains to be said, especially with respect to Pastor Spicer's vision of human fulfillment for the Farrs.

STYLES OF ETHICAL THINKING

By way of preparation for this discussion I want to introduce at this point some distinctions that are widely employed in contemporary moral philosophy. These are distinctions that can help us sort out and better understand different styles of ethical thinking, whether done by theologians, philosophers, ministers, or average people. I am thinking here particularly of the distinction between teleological and deontological ethics that is represented in simplified form in figure A.

By introducing this academic distinction into a book written

Figure A

Some Major Options in Theories of Obligation

Teleological

    1. Ethical egoist

    2. Utilitarian $<\genfrac{}{}{0pt}{}{\text{act}}{\text{rule}}$

Deontological

    1. Divine Command

    2. Existentialist

    3. Kantian

primarily for ministers, I am in effect recommending to clergy readers a knowledge of moral philosophy. Such knowledge of the academic ethical tradition can be helpful especially for those ministers who want to develop a critical practical theology that can function in pluralistic situations in a public way.

Teleological Ethical Views

Moral philosophers make a standard distinction between teleological and deontological methods as two broadly different ways of doing ethics. These are two different ways of answering the question, What are we obligated to do?

If you are a teleologist, you will answer this question by saying that you are obligated to do that act or follow that rule which produces at least as much good over evil as any alternative. Here the catchword is the word *good*. The American philosopher William Frankena, whose definition I am paraphrasing, tells us that the teleologist here would be using "good" in a very specific sense; the reference would be to nonmoral good in contrast to moral good. In his widely read introductory *Ethics* Frankena writes that in order for the teleologist to know what he ought to do, he "must first know what is good in the nonmoral sense and whether the thing in question promotes or is intended to promote what is good in this sense."[6]

By nonmoral good, the teleologist has in mind certain things or qualities that have value, but in other than the strictly moral meaning of "value." We might say that a steak is good. But in saying that, we would not be ascribing any particular moral meanings or qualities to the steak. It is simply good. It tastes good. It is nourishing. It will build our bodies and will probably not hurt us unless we foolishly eat too much of it or already have too much cholesterol in our blood—in which case the steak would be a nonmoral bad in contrast to a nonmoral good. In a similar way we speak of good automobiles, good roads, good houses, good human potentialities (intelligence, creativity, strength), and good experiences (peace, calm, pleasure).

There are subdivisions of the teleological position. If the teleologist feels obligated in his acts to produce more good over evil primarily *for himself*, then he is an "ethical egoist."[7] If the teleologist feels obligated to do that act or follow that rule which will produce the greatest possible balance of good over evil in *the world as a whole*, then he or she is some kind of "utilitarian." The utilitarian is community-oriented whereas the ethical egoist is concerned primarily about the good that accrues to oneself.

Again, utilitarians who are interested primarily in the specific *act* that will lead to the greatest good for the community as a whole are called "act utilitarians" or "situation ethicists." Utilitarians who feel obligated to follow the *rule*—in contrast to the *act*—that will lead to the greatest good for the largest number of people are likely to be called "rule utilitarians."

Finally, there are both secular and religious teleologists and hence both secular and religious ethical egoists and utilitarians. Pastor Spicer seemed to operate at the moral level somewhere between ethical egoism and act utilitarianism.

Deontological Ethical Views

Deontological theories of obligation are generally defined in relation to the teleological theories; that is, the deontologists are seen as denying something the teleologists affirm. What do the deontologists deny? Frankena says: "They deny that the right, the obligatory, and the morally good are wholly, whether directly or indirectly, a function of what is nonmorally good or of what promotes the greatest balance of good over evil for self, one's society, or the world as a whole."[8] The deontologists assert that there are considerations other than the goodness or badness of consequences. These other considerations pertain to certain features of the moral act itself other than the values it promotes. Perhaps it "keeps a promise, is just, or is commanded by God or by the state." Hence, the deontologists say either that nonmoral value consequences are irrelevant to determining our ethical obligations, or that they are not the chief consideration; an act is morally right because of some other fact about it or "because of its own nature."

Here too there are several kinds of deontologists, some secular and some clearly religious. A divine-command deontologist is a person who says that an act is morally right only when it is willed by God and is revealed to the heart either by God's mighty acts in history or by his laws. Another kind of deontologist is a person who says that an act is moral when it exhibits certain features of promise keeping or of justice, and when keeping promises and being just are defined formally and without appeal to the promotion of consequences. Yet another kind of deontologist is the person who says, as do some existentialists, that an act is moral only when it is "authentic," whatever that means. And finally a person is generally thought to be a deontologist if he subscribes to some version of Kant's categorical imperative: "Act only on that maxim which you can at the same time will to be universal law." One's willingness, without reference to consequences, to universalize the principles guiding one's action—this is the supreme mark of a deontologist from a Kantian point of view. Kant and his views are still extremely influential in both secular and religious ethics, particularly in the powerful neo-Kantian moral philosophy of John Rawls and the religious ethics of Ronald Green. Because of their importance for certain aspects of my own position I will have more to say about them later, especially in my discussion of obligation in chapter 6.

Ethical Reflection on Pastor Spicer

What then was the ethical orientation of Pastor Spicer? Is it possible to think about his pastoral care of the Farrs from the perspective of either of these two broad styles of ethical reflection?

Peter Spicer sheds light on his ethical view when he states that it is his ministerial obligation to show forth the love, recognition, and affirmation of God for Jim and Betty Farr. This disclosure, the pastor feels, will help reconstitute their primitive or archaic sense of selfhood and release their powers so they can grow as individuals. Helping the Farrs to maintain the covenants, promises, and pledges inherent in their marriage vows was, to Pastor Spicer, of secondary importance. Strengthening their vulnerable selves, he thought, was the best thing that could be done for Mr. and Mrs. Farr; it was also best for "their family."

In our discussion of teleological ethics a moment ago I suggested that ethically Pastor Spicer could be located somewhere between ethical egoism and act utilitarianism. In terms of what he thought should be done for Jim and Betty, Pastor Spicer appears as an ethical egoist, because their "fulfillment as individuals" seems to be the basic principle controlling his actions. We are not entirely clear what he means by this. But his position appears to be teleological in this sense: their personal fulfillment seems to consist in the actualization of certain inherent potentials or inborn powers. These potentials are nonmoral goods that should be actualized. It is presumed that the love of God finding expression through the church will simultaneously provide security for their fragile selves and activate their individual potentials.

It might appear that Pastor Spicer is an act utilitarian because at one point he does appeal to a larger community good beyond Jim and Betty themselves, namely what is "best for the family." If this is true, then Peter Spicer would be flirting at least with the kind of act utilitarianism or situation ethics associated in theological circles with such names as the Protestant ethicist Joseph Fletcher[9] and the Catholic moral theologian John Giles Milhaven.[10] But even then appeal to the Farrs' family is hardly wide enough in its community reference to identify it as a genuinely act-utilitarian position. If it does approach an act-utilitarian or situation-ethics perspective, however, it does so because of the readiness with which Pastor Spicer is prepared to set aside the covenants, rules, and promises connected with the marriage vows and search for more specific acts that can fulfill the Farrs as individuals, and perhaps fulfill their family as well.

Much more needs to be said about this case from an ethical point of view. And, indeed, we will make reference to the Farrs from time to time in the chapters ahead. But one observation about the relation of Peter Spicer's ethical and psychological interpretations needs to be made now: Pastor Spicer could have developed, even on theological grounds, an alternative ethical perspective, and the moral values guiding his use of Kohut's psychology of the self could have been different than they were. He has other ethical options, and his psychological analysis does not in itself dictate his ethical goals.

He could, for instance, have taken a deontological position, perhaps of the divine-command variety, holding that the commitments of their marriage vows are the primary value for the Farrs, and that these are given by God to be accepted and obeyed. In this view, helping the Farrs overcome their narcissistic disorders and increase their sense of self would serve not so much to free them for actualizing their potentialities as to empower them for affirming and adhering to the marital commitments commanded by God.

And there are other possibilities. Pastor Spicer could have taken a far stronger act-utilitarian or situation-ethics position. His obligation then would have been to emphasize those *acts* which would strengthen Jim and Betty's sense of self so that they could make decisions about their marriage that would produce more good for the general community, not just themselves and their family. Or he could have taken a more rule-oriented perspective, either rule utilitarian or Kantian. I will illustrate later what such positions might mean in the case of the Farrs, and for other kinds of problems.

The point is that the psychological diagnosis and strategy of addressing narcissistic needs can be coupled with a variety of normative understandings about what *should* be the relation between Mr. and Mrs. Farr. And this is true even if, for good pastoral and strategic reasons, Pastor Spicer temporarily brackets—sets aside or puts in the background—his normative view of interpersonal, sexual, and marital relations. There are probably good theological and psychological reasons for not always directly confronting the people we help with the full weight of our normative theological and ethical views. But, even if pastors temporarily bracket them or heuristically set them aside, these views are still always there, necessarily informing what they do in their caring for people. And if the views are still there, then *what* they are—their actual content—must always be a concern. This is true for the sake of ministry, and it should be admitted as true if we are to achieve an adequate understanding of the full dimensions—the full fact—of any helping relation.

It is clear that in recent decades we have not given sufficient attention, in either religious or secular circles, to the full fact of care. In religious contexts, we have tended to emphasize either the normative theological *or* the psychological—and, more and more, *only* the psychological. Our theological-ethical analysis has tended to come in as an afterthought, as it did for Pastor Spicer. Yet the two sides call out for each other. Psychological perspectives are seldom just descriptive, explanatory, and scientific; they almost always have a normative fringe or horizon of their own. And moral-theological or theological-ethical perspectives are never just normative; in addition to pointing to what *should be* the case, they almost always make assumptions about what *is*, thereby moving into descriptive and explanatory modes not unlike psychology and the other sciences.

But these reflections on Pastor Spicer and the case of Jim and Betty Farr raise the question as to how care, both religious and secular, became estranged from the normative disciplines to begin with. This is the question addressed in the following chapter. It will be useful to review this historical development before moving to the more constructive sections of this book where I will attempt to develop a systematic model for relating ethical and psychological perspectives within a larger practical moral theology of care.

CHAPTER 3

The Movement
Toward
Ethical Neutrality

I have been making the point that, in both religious and secular contexts, the trend in care and counseling has been toward greater autonomy—toward independence of the normative disciplines whether of theological ethics or of moral philosophy. So far as the religious context is concerned, this was apparent in the case of Peter Spicer's pastoral care of Jim and Betty Farr. When it came to specifying the ethical perspectives guiding his work, Pastor Spicer's views, in spite of the theological affirmations he attached to them, approximated those of ethical egoism or act utilitarianism. As I will argue later, it is extremely difficult to justify philosophically either ethical-egoist or act-utilitarian interpretations of the major symbols governing the Christian life. Both Joseph Fletcher and John Giles Milhaven have attempted to give an act-utilitarian interpretation to the Christian concepts of love and justice, but their effort has been sharply criticized and widely rejected by theological ethicists.[1]

MINISTERIAL PREFERENCE
FOR PSYCHOLOGICAL MODELS

Many ministers favor act-utilitarian (situation-ethics) interpretations of Christian ethics. Some actually prefer ethical-egoist interpretations of "fulfillment" in the Christian life. This means that when they speak of the goals of the Christian life, these pastors gravitate toward the models found in some psychologies—"self-actualization" or "self-realization"—which are clearly examples of ethical egoism. How did this situation arise whereby clergy and churches of many denominations tend to imitate the values of certain psychologies?

The reasons for this development—sociological, philosophical, psychological—are complex. I will try briefly to clarify a couple of them.

Scientific Neutrality

We noted already in chapter 1 some of the sociological factors that have led psychology and psychiatry to become professional disciplines distinct from philosophy and religion. In addition, there was a strong drive on the part of psychology and psychiatry themselves to become sciences analogous to the hard sciences of physics, chemistry, and biology.

There have always been psychologies—if by psychology we mean certain understandings about how humans function and certain definitions of such things as mind, body, spirit, and soul. Such understandings and definitions are to be found already in both the Hebrew and Christian scriptures and in many other ancient sources as well. The Hebrew distinction between *nephesh* (soul) and *ruach* (spirit) and the New Testament distinctions between *psyche* (soul), *pneuma* (spirit), *nous* (mind), and *sarx* (body) point to kinds of psychologies.[2] But these psychologies were not separated from moral and religious perspectives. Similarly, in the philosophical thought of Plato, Aristotle, Aquinas, and even William James, psychological considerations were distinguished but never isolated from ethical and religious concerns.[3]

Most modern psychologies, however, persisted in wanting to become hard sciences similar to physics, chemistry, and molecular biology. In his early psychoanalytic writings, especially his *Project for a Scientific Psychology* (1895), Freud had such an ambition although it was later tempered.[4] While the model of science was gradually broadened, Freud and other depth psychologists such as Jung, Heinz Hartmann, and David Rapaport still tried to maintain their independence from moral philosophy and theology. Certainly this was a major motive of the more academically based psychologists such as Pavlov, Edward L. Thorndike, Edwin R. Guthrie, Clark L. Hull, and Skinner.

But even though Freud gave up on a psychology modeled after physics and developed instead a medical and psychotherapeutic psychology, he still believed his psychology was neutral and devoid of moral and metaphysical considerations.[5] His much-admired follower Hartmann agreed, saying in his *Psychoanalysis and Moral*

Values that analytic therapy was "a kind of technology." "Science," Hartmann tells us, "cannot decide on what aims one 'ought' to strive for, or what values should be considered supreme. Generally speaking, imperatives cannot logically be deduced from affirmative propositions."[6] This attitude has more or less prevailed. And even though many psychologists and psychiatrists are no longer trying to pattern their discipline after physics and chemistry, they still hope to ground their psychotherapeutic ministrations on the foundations of a neutral science alone.

The desire to enjoy the backing of science is an interest even of those psychologists and psychotherapists who believe that their therapies must be guided by normative views of human fulfillment that have clear moral implications. Carl Rogers, Abraham Maslow, and Fritz Perls, for example, are aware that in their use of Kurt Goldstein's concept of self-actualization as a model of health and human fulfillment they are using a concept that is value-laden and normative. But they believe it is derived from science. The notion that self-actualization of one's inborn potentialities should be the goal of life they regard as a discovery or finding of psychology as science.[7] Here is an interesting case of some psychologists having their cake and eating it too: their normative views of human fulfillment, they believe, are discovered by science; although normative and therefore prescriptive—something they can recommend to everyone—these values are still objective and universally valid because they are uncovered by and grounded in science.

On the other hand, a moral philosopher such as William Frankena would say that Rogers, Maslow, and Perls are deluded. He would contend that the concept of self-actualization is clearly a moral concept—ethical egoism of a nonhedonistic kind.[8] It is nonhedonistic because the main nonmoral values to be actualized are our potentialities—the various biologically grounded powers and gifts that in each person cry out for development—and not some narrow understanding of pleasure, the main nonmoral good espoused by the more hedonistically oriented ethical egoists. Frankena would say that an image of fulfillment such as self-actualization is not grounded in science; it is the personal moral preference of these particular psychologists. Furthermore, the roots of the image go back to ancient Greek philosophies of a eudaemonistic kind, those frequently associated with the names of Plato and Aristotle.[9]

In this regard Erich Fromm is both similar to Rogers, Maslow, and

Perls, and different from them. Like them, Fromm believes that to guide the therapeutic process psychotherapeutic psychology needs a normative image of the human. He presents his concept of the "productive personality" as the appropriate norm, an ideal that is as teleological as the concept of self-actualization, yet far less ethical egoist. In contrast, however, to Maslow, Rogers, and Perls, who contend that their concept of self-actualization derives from science, Fromm is quite clear about the fact that his concept of the productive personality is a philosophical and moral ideal. It is not derived from psychology in the narrow empirical sense of the word, even though psychology plays some role in helping us formulate our normative images.[10] Fromm is unique in acknowledging that he has a normative image of human fulfillment, yet without trying to authenticate it on the basis of empirical psychology.

This brief review of the efforts of psychology and psychiatry to construe themselves as scientifically based may help to clarify the background of the developing dialogue between theology and psychology. As more and more ministers began to read and be influenced by psychology, two things happened. Some ministers, in an effort to compete with psychologists in the helping field, began to imitate the alleged value-neutrality of these disciplines. Other ministers began to acquire and reflect the positive—though supposedly scientifically grounded—value orientations of some psychologists and psychiatrists. Indeed, this may have happened to Pastor Spicer in his own uncomplicated affirmation of the value of self-actualization as a goal of the Christian life.

Fear of Moralism

An additional factor in the drive of therapeutic psychology and psychiatry toward value-neutrality was the fear of moralism. To understand this fear, we must review briefly some of the early theories of neurosis that were espoused by Freud and accepted and developed by others.

As is well known, Freud assigned a particularly crucial role to the harsh, unconscious, and punitive superego in bringing about neurotic reactions in people.[11] Psychoanalysis, he thought, could be successful only if through free association and the therapist's "evenly hovering attention" the censoring superego was led to relax its repressive regime. Freud also saw the superego as the seat of morality. This understanding gave rise to the idea that morality itself, especially civilized sexual morality, was the main source of neurotic suffering.[12]

Later, the highly influential psychotherapeutic and personality theory of Rogers gave support to this view of the role of moral expectations in neurotic dysfunction. Rogers developed the concept of "conditions of worth" as internalizations of parental expectations for good behavior. "Incongruence"—his term for neurosis—comes about when, in order to maintain parental approval, very young children fashion their own self-concepts around their parents' values and expectations that in turn become conditions upon which the worth of their own children is later assigned.[13] Thus incongruence comes about when the child alienates himself from his own experiencing—his own self-actualizing tendencies—and tries to live by somebody else's measure of what is good and proper. Healthy morality, on the contrary, arises only by one's trusting the undistorted felt experience of the total organism. "Out of this complex weighing and balancing" on the part of the total organism, a person is able "to discover that course of action which seems to come closest to satisfying all his needs in the situation, long-range as well as immediate needs."[14]

Thus, for Rogers, getting beyond moralism really means in effect to accept a particular type of moral outlook: morality is reduced to satisfying one's own needs. Clearly, this is the particular ethical position we have called ethical egoism. It is one that is shared by other humanistic psychologists. Ethical egoism is not a moral position demanded by science, but a philosophical-moral position imputed to science.

The question naturally arises: Is this the only moral position that is consistent with avoiding the pitfalls of moralism? I think not, even though Pastor Spicer, it would appear, believes that it is.

AVOIDING MORALISM
IN PASTORAL THEOLOGY

It is through this fear of moralism that modern psychotherapeutic psychology has done the most to influence today's ministry, especially in the mainline churches. To see how this has happened, it may be helpful to look at certain widely read writings of two of our best-known contemporary pastoral theologians, Seward Hiltner and Howard Clinebell.

Both Hiltner and Clinebell are appreciative of the contributions of modern psychotherapeutic psychology. They are especially interested in what it has taught us about the problem of moralism—which in their own pastoral theology and pastoral counseling they seek to avoid. They do not, by any means, go to the extremes of Freud and Hartmann. They do not feign neutrality, and they know that the larger role of the minister as religious and moral leader can never be excluded from any helping relationship. Nonetheless—and despite the important differences between them—serious questions can be raised about both Hiltner and Clinebell. Their difficulties can be summarized as follows: (1) a tendency to romanticize the ethical resources of individuals; (2) a failure to recognize the extent to which moral pluralism exists in our culture, both inside and outside the church; and (3) a failure to recognize that for ethics to be relevant to pastoral care it must go beyond confessionalism and have critical depth. Hiltner is especially susceptible to the first charge. The second and third pertain to both Hiltner and Clinebell, though the third is especially applicable to Clinebell.

Seward Hiltner

In his early and still widely used *Pastoral Counseling* (1949) Hiltner states that intentional or unintentional moralism is one of the most serious dangers in the minister's care and counseling. "In counseling," he tells us, "moral judgments in place of understanding and clarification are especially likely to be disastrous."[15] Note that Hiltner does not say there is no role whatever for moral judgments anywhere in the pastor's ministry. On the contrary: "We preach about the criteria of right and wrong, and properly so." The problem arises when the minister's moral commitments get in the way of understanding. This can occur especially in the early phases of any caring or counseling relationship. Furthermore, the pastor should not be anxious to announce his own moral perspective because generally this is "already fairly clear from the noncounseling aspects of his work." This statement, I believe, is an example of Hiltner's failure to recognize the extent of the ethical pluralism that exists today, even within the church and between pastor and congregation.

Hence, Hiltner tells us that the minister should set aside personal moral convictions in the context of care and counseling. He believes that the proper goal is to assist persons to become more autonomous in their ethics. Counseling should be "eductive"; that is, it should lead or draw "more and more of the solution to the situation out of the creative potentialities of the person needing help."[16] Both counseling and precounseling are eductive: "Both leave it up to the parishioner—after certain things are done." The parishioner's "right to be responsible for, and to run, his own life are held to throughout."[17] Hence, although Hiltner avoids the overt neutrality typical of some of the secular helping professions, he takes a step in that direction. In simultaneously setting aside the minister's moral values and attempting to stay totally within the value framework of the parishioner, he is certainly moving toward neutrality and perhaps moral relativism.

Later, in his *Preface to Pastoral Theology* (1958), Hiltner makes an important distinction between pastoral theology and moral theology or theological ethics. The latter disciplines are "logic centered" in contrast to pastoral theology which is "operation centered."[18] Since pastoral theology, for Hiltner, deals with the "shepherding perspective" or the care and counseling functions of ministry, this distinction places pastoral care into an ambiguous situation so far as its relation to moral theology and theological ethics is concerned. First of all, it is not at all clear that moral theology and theological ethics are only "logic-centered disciplines." They deal with the norms of practice; rightly conceived, they are the practical theological disciplines par excellence. They must be the organizing center even of pastoral care and counseling as kinds of ministerial practice.

Failure to understand this leads Hiltner to adopt a situation (or act-utilitarian) ethic. Ministerial work, he contends, must be guided by two kinds of ethic, one for the individual and one for the larger community. Pastoral awareness of the situation determines which the pastor should subscribe to at any given moment. If the dominant need, "as made necessary by the situation, is toward the protection or purity or general welfare of the community," then some kind of communal ethic should obtain. If the dominant need, "as made necessary by the situation, is toward enhancing the welfare and the good of the person," then a more individual ethic is in order.[19]

This seems to pit pastoral care and counseling against communal ethics. Indeed, the problem is further compounded when Hiltner characterizes pastoral work with individuals as completely eductive, as always involved with the leading out of "something that may be regarded as either within the person or potentially available to him."[20] Even though we cannot be altogether sure what this means, on its face it seems to leave Hiltner dangerously close to an ethical egoism not unlike that of Pastor Spicer. For we must remember that even an act-utilitarian or situation ethic is finally an ethic for the community—an ethic designed to maximize good over evil for humankind in general. Hence, not even a Christian act utilitarian such as Fletcher can have both an ethic for individuals and an ethic for the community. In the end there is only one ethic—the communal ethic. Certain exceptions might upon occasion be made to the community ethic, but even these exceptions are made on its behalf—which is to say that in the long run the exception is seen to be the best (Christians would say the most loving) thing to do for both the individual and the community—in fact the best thing for the individual precisely as member of the community.

Howard Clinebell

Hiltner, who has done more for practical and pastoral theology than any other living theologian, can at least be commended for actually discussing the questions of ethics in pastoral care and counseling. Many of his contemporaries hardly mention the subject. In the work of Howard Clinebell another step is taken toward reclaiming a closer relation between pastoral care and theological ethics. The step, however, is hesitant at best.

Clinebell has contributed to pastoral care and counseling a new and more complex model—one that he calls a "revised model."[21] This is a model that still affirms and to some extent uses the "client-centered" insight and orientations of Freud and Rogers that Hiltner also employs in his eductive counseling. But Clinebell's model goes beyond these others by emphasizing the need, upon many occasions, to take a more supportive, reality-confronting, future-oriented, information-giving, positive, and actional approach in care and counseling. Much of the time Clinebell talks about this in more or less technical terms by recommending that the minister help people to "cope," to "confront reality," and to accentuate their "positive personality resources," and also give them "information" or "suggestions." At such times, Clinebell's writing takes on the neutral and technicist tones of much of contemporary secular psychotherapeutic psychology, with all of its striving to be scientific, all of its fear of moralism. But in one highly important chapter in his widely used *Basic Types of Pastoral Counseling* (1966) Clinebell does develop an argument for introducing ethical concerns directly into counseling. He argues for the role of moral confrontation in counseling. At one point he boldly asserts: "The minister should never be timid in counseling about what he regards as right."[22]

Clinebell makes use of the psychotherapeutic psychology of O. Hobart Mowrer and William Glasser to argue that many people suffer from repressed guilt rather than repressed instinctuality. Such individuals can be helped only by having their guilt confronted and acknowledged. Insight therapies or uncovering therapies that emphasize early childhood experiences may miss the point. Clinebell approvingly tells the story of a pastor counseling with a man who was having an affair with his secretary. He writes that the minister "firmly helped him face the destructive consequences of his irresponsible behavior for himself, his children, and his wife. This mobilized his appropriate guilt. The pastor then supported the side of the man which wanted to break off the exotic but damaging relationship."[23] This vigorous moral confrontation on the part of the minister apparently gave the man a positive way of handling his real guilt. Such an approach need not be moralistic, Clinebell suggests, if the pastor does it with real love, profound acceptance, and genuine affirmation of the basic personhood of the people with whom he works.

All of Clinebell's argument is full of possibilities and needs to be taken seriously. But his example of the minister taking a firm and authoritative moral stand with the sexually errant man has three difficulties: (1) It assumes with respect to sexual matters a fundamental agreement between minister and lay people that may not actually exist, failing to recognize the pluralism that frequently does exist and the difficulties of working through such fundamental disagreements as may arise. (2) It assumes that the pastor can simply assert his point of view in a precritical and prereflective way. This is often possible, especially when shared assumptions actually exist. But when they do not, then a more rational, critical, and public approach to ethics, even theological ethics, needs to be available. In saying this, however, I must quickly add that the question of how to handle a more reflective ethic within the context of a caring relation is another issue, one that I will return to more than once in this book. (3) On the basis of what is reported about the psychological dynamics involved, we really do not know enough about this man to say for sure that repressed guilt is his real problem and needs to be handled in this specific way. Men have affairs with their secretaries for a great variety of dynamic reasons. Before we can, with Clinebell, endorse this kind of direct and immediate moral confrontation, we need to know more than Clinebell tells us about the person involved.

Although Clinebell is clearly moving in the right direction, he falls considerably short of where we must go. On the one hand, he does not present us with a thoroughly reflective and critical practical moral theology to address such situations of care. And on the other hand, he does not give us a thoroughly dynamic understanding of this and other cases. He is neither sufficiently theological nor sufficiently psychological. Only when we become more self-conscious about both perspectives can more specific practical issues of timing and strategy in relating them be addressed.

CHAPTER 4

Trends in Protestant and Catholic Ethics

Pastoral care and counseling, we have said, needs to be grounded in a practical moral theology or theological ethics, more than has been the case in recent decades. In the present social context, as I am painfully aware, this is easier to say than to do clearly and effectively. The statement itself, moreover, seems to assume that moral theology and theological ethics are reasonably clear and coherent disciplines, which may not be the case.

THE COMPLEXITY OF THE DISCIPLINES

Disciplines that deal with the norms of action are exceedingly complex, dynamic, and difficult to make precise. As my colleague Stephen Toulmin has pointed out, ethics, whether religious or secular, is a discipline of this kind.[1] Certainly Protestant theological ethics and Catholic moral theology both exhibit such complexities and instabilities. James Gustafson discusses some of them in his *Protestant and Roman Catholic Ethics*. In fact, there are strong tendencies in both these ethical traditions that are now pushing them toward relativism, situationalism, and historicism. To put it differently, there are strong forces pushing both these traditions toward some of the situational and relativistic values we have seen to be implicit in the social and psychological disciplines themselves.

Curricular Disjunction

First, it should be acknowledged that theological ethics in Protestant divinity schools, as a discipline distinct from systematic theology, is a rather recent phenomenon. It is probably only since Walter Rauschenbusch that theological ethics began to appear as a separate offering in the curriculum of Protestant divinity. In this respect Catholic moral theology is a much older and more stable tradition.

Ethics and Penance

Moreover, in the Catholic tradition pastoral care, understood primarily as the administration of the sacrament of penance, has always had a direct and intimate connection with moral theology. In order to administer absolution the priest had to be an ethicist and moral theologian. He had to have a moral perspective out of which to determine the severity of moral sins, calculate penances, and grant forgiveness. To this extent Catholicism and Judaism have had more in common with each other than either has had with Protestantism. Gustafson writes:

> It is not unreasonable to suggest that this role of the priest is more similar historically to one aspect of the office of the rabbi in traditional Judaism than it is to the role of the Protestant minister. Both the priest and the rabbi function as teachers of morality. They are instructors of their congregations in the requirements of morality and, indeed, of moral law. . . . To make judgments, both the priest and the rabbi exercise their capacities to reason—granted, in quite different ways. . . . Rabbinic rationality and logic are parallel in function to the rationality of canon lawyers and moral theologians. Law, on the whole, has not had a similar centrality in Protestant history.[2]

Since the time of the Reformation, however, there has been little comparable interest in the sacrament of penance amongst Protestants. "Justification by grace through faith" and *sola gratia* have made them skeptical both of the category of the law and of any rational attempt to discern it, measure people by it, or implement it. There are exceptions, of course, to this general rule. The Anglican tradition has at times kept alive confession and penance and a tradition of moral theology. The Puritan tradition, though its clergy did not have priestly authority to forgive sins, has wrestled with "cases of conscience." The Anabaptists and Methodists had firm practical moralities and methods for examining conscience in their small-group life.[3] On the whole, however, Protestants have emphasized sin in general rather than particular sins, and practiced general corporate confession within the context of worship rather than specific individual confession in either public or private forms. In the main there has always been in Protestantism an ambivalent relationship between pastoral care and serious theological ethics.

INHERITED DEFICIENCIES

Both Protestant and Catholic ethics in recent decades have become conscious of certain inherited weaknesses. Indeed, they have been making concerted efforts to overcome the deficiencies.

Catholic Moral Theology

Traditionally, Catholic moral theology has tended to make ethical pronouncements on the basis of deductions from a rationally developed philosophical anthropology. This anthropology gave a prominent place both to the results of natural reason and to the structure and *telos* of natural human inclinations. It was a natural-law ethic. The natural law reflects the mind of God. The mind of God, it was assumed, reveals itself both in Holy Scripture and in other natural structures and inclinations, including human reason.

Because of its confidence in reason's capacity to deduce immutable moral laws from the knowable ends of nature (for example, procreation as the major goal of sexuality), traditional Catholic moral theology has in recent decades been criticized as being physicalistic, biologistic, undynamic, nonhistorical, and unconsciously culture-bound. It has used its vast intellectual resources, some argue, only to end up affirming a wide range of traditional and outdated Catholic moral customs, especially in the area of sexuality—the most widely known of course being the perennial Catholic positions on contraception and abortion.

In view of these static and nonhistorical tendencies, it is not surprising that modern methods of Catholic pastoral care and counseling, influenced as they are by the therapies of acceptance and the insights of dynamic psychology, have attempted to separate themselves as much as possible from the strictures of traditional Catholic moral theology. On the whole, when Catholicism began to sprout its own brand of pastoral psychologists, people such as Charles Curran and Eugene Kennedy, these people separated themselves as much as possible from the traditional moral theology framework.

Catholic moral theology is generally seen to have the structure of a teleological ethic. It bears the marks of all teleological ethics in that moral obligation is determined ultimately with reference to the bringing into existence of the nonmoral good, the *summum bonum*. This is why Catholic moral theology historically has been so interested in the structure and *telos* of our natural human tendencies and affections.

Protestant Theological Ethics

Protestant theological ethics, on the other hand, up until the twentieth century has been far more deontological—an ethic of the divine command as revealed in Scripture. This divine command may consist of little more than "love thy neighbor," as with Luther. For him, the command comes primarily as gift and grace, and our response is a matter of gratitude. In more scholastic or conservative forms of Protestantism the command may also include the Old Testament decalogue as well as the specific teachings of Jesus and of the New Testament writers.

There was little place for moral reason or philosophical anthropology in the early Protestant sources, Calvin being perhaps an exception. Calvin emphasized continuity and commensurability between the Old Testament, Jesus, and the New Testament on the one hand and the natural moral law written in the hearts of humans on the other hand. In the *Institutes* he writes, "That inward law [the natural law], which we have described as written, even engraved, upon the hearts of all, in a sense asserts the very same things that are learned from the Two Tables."[4] Gustafson, in commenting on this ecumenical breadth of Calvin, makes the following observation: "This marks a continuity with the Roman Catholic tradition (which, incidentally, suggests that constructive ecumenical ethics done from the perspective of Protestantism might best begin with Calvin)."[5]

In recent decades Protestant theological ethics has had to face problems quite different from the deductivism, physicalism, and static nature of the traditional manuals in Catholic moral theology. Historicism and relativism have recently been major features of much Protestant theological ethics. Its divine-command ethics has frequently degenerated into either act-deontological or act-utilitarian points of view. Fearful of anything resembling justification by works or justification by adherence to the law, Protestant ethics has shied away from any method that would articulate general principles which might reasonably appeal to people outside of the Christian fold. The dominant model proposed by many of the major Protestant thinkers of the twentieth century has focused on God's specific acts in history as apprehended in the existential or historical moment through the faith of the individual Christian. The concern of the Christian, then, is to determine how God is acting in history, and on the whole to do this without the aid of moral reason or philosophical anthropology.

Gustafson finds that to be the primary model in the European neo-orthodoxy of Barth and Bultmann, in the Americans H. Richard Niebuhr and Paul Lehmann, and in many of the more fashionable liberation theologians. In this kind of model, a single idea such as *agape*, known through God's acts in history, often becomes the only guiding ethical principle. Such ethical orientations frequently become occasional, episodic, and relativistic. God does different things at different points in history, and the dictates of love seem to vary accordingly from moment to moment.

Strangely enough, even though the starting point is clearly deontological, grounded in the command and will of God, there frequently begins to emerge quite soon a subtle or not-so-subtle utilitarianism or situation ethics, the idea that we know God's action by its consequences. The consequences of God's actions are either loving (Joseph Fletcher, John Giles Milhaven, H. Richard Niebuhr), or humanizing (Lehmann), or liberating (Gustavo Gutierrez, Juan L. Segundo). As Gustafson points out, such loving—or humanizing or liberating as the case may be—then becomes a specification of the good. Protestant theological ethics has then evolved into a consequentialism—situational, occasionalistic, and relativistic to be sure but teleological nonetheless.

This is precisely where Pastor Spicer ended up in his own work with Jim and Betty. Beginning with a deontological starting point in the love of God, his ethic ended in a teleological consequentialism, one that was more ethical egoist than utilitarian. Because of Pastor Spicer's profound interest in psychology, we have assumed that he got part of his teleology and ethical egoism from the values of self-actualization associated with humanistic psychology. We can assume too, perhaps, that this may also be a source for his lack of interest in moral principles and rules, though our brief characterization of contemporary moral theology and theological ethics demonstrates that there is today, especially in Protestant moral thought, a trend toward disdain for general moral principles and rules and a movement in the direction of an ethic of consequence.

Is there, then, a subtle reinforcement and congruence between certain types of psychology and certain types of theological ethics? And if so, is this good? Is the right kind of ethics evolving to guide our care and counseling?

THE NEED FOR METHOD
IN ETHICS

This is the task that confronts us in this book: How do we relate moral theology or theological ethics to dynamic psychology for purposes of guiding pastoral care and counseling? How can these two disciplines be brought together effectively so as to provide norms for our practical acts of care while at the same time avoiding moralism?

It is my contention that in order for this to happen, theological ethics itself must have a better method. This method, for both Catholic and Protestant ethics, should specify the role of tradition (both Scripture and church history), the role of reason and experience, and the role of the other disciplines of the human (especially sociology and dynamic psychology). Only an ethic that combines these three elements will avoid moralism.

The ethic I hope to develop here will be ecumenical, using parts of both Catholic moral theology and Protestant theological ethics. Catholic moral theology has been strong in its use of tradition, reason, and experience but weak in its use of Scripture and the social sciences. Protestant theological ethics has been stronger in its use of Scripture and of both sociology and psychology but weaker in its use of tradition, reason, and experience. Yet if we analyze our actual moral deliberations it is my conviction that all of us, knowingly or not, use all of these sources. The trick is to understand how and why. This will be our task in the next two chapters.

CHAPTER 5

Method in Practical Moral Thinking

In its practice of care the church historically has confidently affirmed a host of understandings—attitudes about which it is considerably more cautious today. In the past the church always said that the sick should be healed and the elderly respected and maintained, that the starving should be fed, and the ill kept alive, that genital sexuality should be confined to marriage, and that suicide is a sin. Today, however, in one way or another there is deep conflict and discussion about each of these issues, even among those who call themselves Christians.

While the reader may not be puzzling over these issues, the questions are far from settled in the minds of many people, both inside and outside the church. Addressing such questions is clearly a part of the full task—the full fact—of ministry and pastoral care. To be a pastoral theologian today—what I have called a critical practical moral theologian of care—is to think hard about such issues theoretically and to develop action strategies for addressing them. But in order to achieve this we must have available to us adequate methods for doing practical moral reflection.

METHOD FOR THE COMMUNITY

The method of practical moral thinking to be outlined in this book is not intended for the exclusive knowledge and use of the minister. Method is a matter for the whole congregation and, indeed, the larger church as well.

The Church as Community of Moral Discourse

The model of the church to be used here, as in my earlier *Moral Context of Pastoral Care*, is that of the church as a community of moral discourse, a model first elaborated by my colleague James Gustafson.[1] This model is perhaps best elaborated by utilizing two of the five models set forth so clearly by Avery Dulles in his *Models of the Church*—specifically the church as herald and the church as servant. This is not to say that his other models—the church as institution, as mystical communion, and as sacrament—are irrelevant. They are ever-present themes, but subordinate in this context to those of the church as herald and as servant.

As a model, the church as servant carries with it many of the values of the church as herald. In the image of the church as herald—an image central to most of Protestant Christianity—one finds the idea of the Church as gathered by and proclaimer of God's Word about the future coming of his kingdom.[2] But this proclaiming or heralding of the coming of God's righteous reign is accomplished basically through servanthood—the servanthood of Jesus and the servanthood or *diakonia* of his disciples. In fact, this servanthood is the first sign of the coming of the kingdom. Dulles calls this view—the church as servant—a "secular-dialogical" model. By this he means that the church guides the world (by pointing to the kingdom) and listens to the world, thereby serving the world. This view of the church acknowledges the relative autonomy of the various aspects of culture—science, art, government—and both respects their inner *telos* and criticizes their idolatries and distortions.

In a secular and highly pluralistic culture this model of the church can be carried forward only when the church is self-consciously a community of moral discourse. The model assumes both the immanence of God in creation, including the various expressions of culture, and a critical transcendence of God over all aspects of the created world, including its various cultures and even the church itself. But the criticisms that the church brings to the world are not mysterious and opaque; they are intelligible—even if not always immediately intelligible—to general human consciousness. On such a view the church is permitted to enter into public conversation with a view to the creation of a truly human society, even if that society is not always explicitly Christian in all respects.

The church as a community of practical moral discourse is not cut off from its religious foundations. After all, this community has certain beliefs about the ultimate nature of the world and about God who is the foundation of that world, and these beliefs have relevance for practical moral rationality. But by moral discourse, moral thinking, or practical rationality I have in mind something more than a restatement of the church's beliefs. I am thinking of something very broad, more inclusive even than narrow technical rationality or, for that matter, narrowly conceived moral reasoning as such. What I envision is a hermeneutical rationality.

Hermeneutics as Conversation

Hermeneutics refers to the process of interpretation and the rules that govern it. Interpretation is a process, as Richard Palmer says, of "bringing to understanding," of making "familiar, present, and comprehensible" the meaning of something that is other or foreign.[3] A hermeneutical process is necessary for understanding the depths of one's own faith, and a hermeneutical process is necessary for understanding the perspectives and meanings of the other people we confront in a pluralistic society. As Hans-Georg Gadamer,[4] David Tracy,[5] and Richard Rorty[6] have contended, hermeneutics is basically a conversation. And it is within this model of hermeneutics as conversation that I want to place my theory of practical moral rationality.

PRACTICAL MORAL RATIONALITY

Our goal is to discover some kind of moral theory that can guide our attempts to care and counsel one another. To pursue that goal is to face two inevitable questions: What kind of theory do we want? What is the relation of theory to practice?

Theory and Practice

My view is that theory arises out of practice and leads back to practice. Theory (*theoria*) is an abstraction from and reflection of practice (*praxis*).[7] Praxis is the basic or prior reality. The test of good theory is largely the adequacy with which it guides practice. Our theoretical knowledge always comes out of prior practice, prior participation, and prereflective involvement with the practical activities of living communities. The knowledge found in theory is always preceded by prereflective participatory knowledge, something close to what the ancient Hebrews had in mind with the word *yada* (to know or experience, as in Gen. 4:1).

The theory-practice connection I have in mind is close to that stated recently by Tom Groome in his *Christian Religious Education*.[8] What he says there about a "shared praxis" approach to religious education is equally applicable to the church as a community of care. In both cases we should picture a community of life together (in this case the church) sharing some ongoing activity or practice. Its activity or practice is interrupted by some problem, issue, or crisis that forces the community to start thinking or reflecting about its practice. The issue could be one involving its educational practice, its care practice, its mission practice, or its maintenance practice. In reflecting, the community reexamines and reinterprets its history, its major symbols, its past commitments, and other aspects of its life in order to come up with a hypothesis or theory about the right way to proceed with its action. If this community exists in a pluralistic society, and if part of its problem involves a conflict between its agenda and that of another community, then its reflection may also have to entail appreciative interpretation and criticism of the other community's history, major symbols, and basic commitments.

A Revised Correlational Method

What is entailed here is a "revised correlational method" for doing practical theology. The approach is applicable to all forms of practical theology. It certainly applies to the task of establishing a practical moral theology of care. This approach to theology is associated with the names Daniel Day Williams, Seward Hiltner, and Tracy among others. It has received powerful expression in Tracy's *Blessed Rage for Order* and *The Analogical Imagination.*[9]

In general terms a revised correlational program in practical theology attempts to correlate critically those questions and answers that are derived from various interpretations of the central Christian witness with those questions and answers that are implicit in various interpretations of ordinary human experience. In its correlation of one set of questions and answers with another set of questions and answers this method is different from Paul Tillich's method of correlation, which correlates questions from existence with answers from revelation. The revised correlational method as applied to a practical moral theology means a critical correlation between such norms for human action and fulfillment as are revealed in interpretations of the Christian witness and those norms for human action and fulfillment that are implicit in various interpretations of ordinary human experience. The emphasis is thus upon correlating critically various *interpretations* of the norms of action and fulfillment; one never has access either to the pristine Christian event or to raw uninterpreted experience. This is why even a practical theology is always a hermeneutical process.

This method, already extended into practical theology in the religious education theory of Groome, has been utilized by James and Evelyn Whitehead in their general theory of ministerial reflection, *Method in Ministry*. The Whiteheads are particularly helpful in that they differentiate Tracy's concept of ordinary experience into cultural experience on the one hand and personal experience on the other. By cultural experience they mean literature, the social sciences, popular culture, or any other perspective that tries to interpret ordinary experience. In addition to theological and cultural interpretations the Whiteheads introduce the category of personal experience.[10] They readily admit that our personal experience will include elements of both religious heritage and cultural interpretation, but they also insist that the unique synthesis which is our own personal experience should be regarded as a distinct interpretative perspective in the task of critical correlation. Practical theological reflection for the Whiteheads thus entails a complex process of critically correlating interpretations from three distinct sources—tradition, culture, and personal experience. By this inclusion of personal experience, they have developed a framework for incorporating within a systematic practical theology some of the emphases and methodologies of clinical pastoral education and the case method approach to theological reflection.

But the Whiteheads, Groome, and Tracy are not specific enough about the actual steps necessary for doing a *critical* correlation. They do not go far enough in helping us actually to establish our norms of action and fulfillment—norms that are crucial for guiding all forms of practical action but especially practical action designed to care for and counsel people. The Whiteheads helpfully suggest that practical theological method has three stages or moments—the stage of attention or listening, the stage of assertion, and the stage of decision.[11] The stage of attending, of course, is basically the hermeneutical stage in which we listen to and interpret (following the best hermeneutical principles available) the various perspectives involved. The stage of assertion is a time to assert one's own perspective and critically compare it with that of others. But this is precisely where the Whiteheads' important contribution breaks down. They provide no concrete method for actually controlling the critical and comparative task at the stage of assertion. Hence no proper basis is laid for moving on to the stage of decision.

A slight revision and extension is needed in their threefold understanding of the stages of practical theological action. There are really four steps in the process: (1) the experience of the problem, (2) attention and listening, (3) critical analysis and comparison, and (4) decision and strategy. In chapter 6 I will describe five levels of practical moral rationality that are relevant to all four of these steps, but especially to the highly crucial third step of critical analysis and comparison.

METHOD AND PASTOR SPICER

A revised correlational approach to a practical moral theology would have helped Peter Spicer in his work with Jim and Betty Farr. Pastor Spicer tends to use both Christian theology and Heinz Kohut's self-psychology (with a dash of humanistic psychology thrown in to help define the goals of human fulfillment). He derives his norms for action and his image of human fulfillment from three sources—Christian tradition, contemporary culture (in the form of certain psychologies), and personal experience. Although we do not have much information about his personal experience, it is clear from his affirmation of a kind of ethical egoism as the norm for Mr. and Mrs. Farr that Pastor Spicer's personal experience was aligned with the image of human fulfillment found in many modern psychologies. Not all, but many of the modern psychologies are guided by an implicit ethical egoism. They may claim to be neutral about such values as human fulfillment, or to have grounded their particular views on science, but there are reasons to remain skeptical on both counts.

Who then is right? Is the Christian view of human fulfillment as *agape* and self-transcendence to be automatically endorsed? Can anything be said for ethical egoism? Christians are disposed by faith to regard human fulfillment in terms of *agape*. But if they are functioning within a pluralistic situation, then these same Christians will be pressed to do the following: (1) specify what they really mean by *agape;* (2) give reasons for its "relative adequacy" (to borrow a phrase from Tracy),[12] its assumed superiority over ethical-egoist views; (3) state what can be positively affirmed about ethical-egoist views such as those aiming at self-realization or self-actualization; and (4) articulate feasible strategies for actually moving people toward greater *agape* without at the same time causing them to break under the weight of spiraling expectations. If Pastor Spicer attempts to do these things, he will be adopting a revised correlational approach to a practical moral theology that will guide his care and counseling of people.

CHAPTER 6

The Five Levels of Practical Moral Thinking

All practical moral thinking has a religious dimension to it, whether or not this is consciously acknowledged. Not all moral thinking, however, is explicitly Christian in its religious orientation. Because all moral thinking has a religious dimension or horizon, it is possible to argue that all caring disciplines, even secular ones, in their efforts to articulate their images of human fulfillment must somehow be undergirded by a practical morality that is also religious. Hence all caring disciplines—even modern psychiatry, psychology, and social work—have behind them a religious ethic, though not necessarily a Christian ethic.

THE FIVE QUESTIONS
IN MORAL REFLECTION

Now, there are five levels of practical moral thinking. This is true for any kind of moral thinking, whether it be explicitly religious or not. The five levels of practical moral rationality follow from the five primary questions we invariably ask ourselves, whether consciously or unconsciously, when circumstances force a moral issue upon us. The questions are phrased here as they would be put, not to individuals, but to communities, and especially to the church as a community of moral discourse: (1) What kind of world or universe constitutes the ultimate context of our action? (2) What are we obligated to do? (3) Which of all our human tendencies and needs are we morally justified in satisfying? (4) What is the immediate context of our action and the various factors which condition it? (5) What specific roles, rules, and processes of communication should we follow in order to accomplish our moral ends?

These five questions reveal the structure of all moral action, whether that action is pursued by an individual or a community. They open up the five levels of practical moral thinking, levels which are hierarchical yet mutually dependent upon one another. The first question, for instance, opens up the religious, or what can be called the metaphorical, level of practical moral rationality. It asks questions and demands answers about the ultimate context of experience—whether our world or universe is basically trustworthy or untrustworthy, warm or cold, responsive or indifferent. More specific questions of moral obligation always end up, sooner or later, making assumptions at this level. Answers at this most fundamental level are always presupposed at each of the other four levels. Yet the four lower levels of moral concern are never completely determined in their content by this first level of concern. And in order for moral reflection to be complete, all of the lower levels are required. The first alone does not suffice.

All of this admittedly sounds quite abstract. In most of its care and counseling the Christian community does not become quite so analytic. Indeed, to do so is generally not necessary and, at times, could be destructive. In addition, it can be the very essence of moralism for a pastor or anyone else to become analytic when what is needed is tender concern, presence, and empathy. Why then go through this analytic exercise involving five levels of thinking? The answer is simple: we do it in order to straighten out our confusion when we get in a muddle. And if the five-level framework that follows has any validity, it is not that the minister should come across as an expert who uses it in order to provide answers for less-sophisticated people. Our analysis proceeds in order to provide a method that congregations as a whole can gradually learn to utilize in their deliberations together—communally exercising their divinely ordained powers for practical rationality to provide a contextual background for their care of one another and of the world. Such care must be exercised with humility and tenderness and with an acute sense of human—and Christian—fallibility. But it also should be exercised with confidence that progress can be made. Our care and counseling can be improved.

THE FIVE LEVELS OF
PRACTICAL MORAL THINKING

The five questions generate five levels of practical moral thinking. These can be identified as follows: (1) a metaphorical level, (2) an obligational level, (3) a tendency-need level, (4) a contextual-predictive level, and (5) a rule-role level.

The metaphorical level deals with the various metaphorical and symbolic ways we use to represent the ultimate context of experience; it is the most distinctively and formally religious level, although practical religions always have convictions and make judgments and statements at all five levels. The obligational level is the most distinctively moral level. The tendency-need level tries to answer the question as to what humans want and what they need and value—in the nonmoral (although not necessarily immoral) sense of those terms. The contextual-predictive level tries to specify the common sociological, psychological, and cultural trends which are likely to condition our actions and their consequences. And finally, the rule-role level tries to articulate the concrete rules, roles, and processes of communication necessary to construct a world according to the visions, obligations, and possibilities opened up at the higher levels.

In our day the disciplines of theology have tended to specialize at these different levels, with no single discipline or subdiscipline responsible for integrating them all systematically. This may be why theology has lost some of its intellectual power in guiding the church—why theology is often said to be abstract and irrelevant. Insofar as any one theological specialty addresses just one of these levels and ignores the others it is indeed abstract: it has abstracted out an important level but ignored all the rest. It has failed to attend to the "full fact" of human action and human decision making. It is irrelevant mainly because it is incomplete.

In recent decades philosophical or fundamental theology and systematic theology have specialized at the metaphorical level. They have concentrated on testing the truth of religious metaphors (philosophical theology) or on uncovering their meaning (systematic theology and its preoccupation with hermeneutics). Moral theology and theological ethics have concerned themselves primarily with the obligational level. The various practical theologies have specialized on the last three levels—the tendency-need, contextual-predictive, and rule-role levels. These practical theologies are often criticized for failing to attend to the more foundational metaphorical and obligational levels; they are seen as shallow and superficial. On the other hand, because philosophical, systematic, and moral theologies fail to address the three lower levels, they are seen as abstract and irrelevant. Both sets of judgments, I fear, are basically correct. To do its task fully, theology must eventually operate at all five levels. If it does, it can be thoroughly practical. Any theology that wishes to have the luxury of not addressing all of these levels (and there are certainly good reasons for specialization) must openly and humbly admit its incompleteness.

The Levels and Correlation

Before sketching the content of the five levels, I need to say just a word about their role in relation to the revised correlational task of practical theology. The hermeneutical task is to uncover and interpret what a particular tradition has to say at each of the five levels. If, for example, we are interpreting early Christianity, the writings of Paul, or the contributions of Irenaeus, we should be prepared to uncover what we can for each of the five levels. Frequently we will discover that the same author does not address all five levels and that the author's assumptions about some of the levels are either implicit or unclear. We will also learn that the first two or three levels rightfully have the greater importance for us. What the New Testament writers say about our universe, our obligations, and our basic human needs (levels one, two, and three) has the largest claim on us as listeners to their words. Their thoughts and assumptions about their own social and cultural contexts and about concrete roles and rules (levels four and five) are more variable, more contingent, and more subject to creative reworking by us, the appropriators.

But truly to address the revised correlational task of practical theology, one would need to interpret the central witness of the Judeo-Christian tradition at each of these various levels, then interpret various other competing cultural interpretations of ordinary experience at these same five levels, and, finally—the critical task— conduct a public conversation between the central witness of the Judeo-Christian tradition and the current cultural perspective in an effort to discern the "relative adequacy" of the two perspectives. This formulation of the task implies an acknowledgment that God's world is one world, and that the truth can be found in a variety of places, not just within the discernible confines of the witnessing Christian community.

If one's personal experience is also to be allowed into the conversation, it too would need to be analyzed in relation to the same five levels. The critical correlation would then become a three-way conversation. Personal experience would submit to interpretation and criticism by the other two perspectives, and would itself in turn interpret and criticize them—both the religious tradition and the cultural perspective. This would be the way to accomplish what clinical pastoral education is supposed to be all about.

And now, one last preliminary remark: there are both objective and subjective aspects to these five levels. From the subjective side, to be discussed in chapter 8, they form the grounds of a dispositional ethic, helping us to analyze character and virtue and to answer the question, Who is the good person? The objective, subjective (characterological or aretical) and personal perspectives on moral thinking are represented in figure B.

Figure B

The Triangle of Practical Moral Thinking

Objective ———————— Characterological (Aretaic)

Objective	Characterological (Aretaic)
1. Metaphorical	1. Faith Development
2. Obligational	2. Moral Development
3. Tendency-Need	3. Emotional-Motivational Development
4. Contextual-Predictive	4. Ego Development (Reality Perception)
5. Rule-Role	5. Rule-Role Development

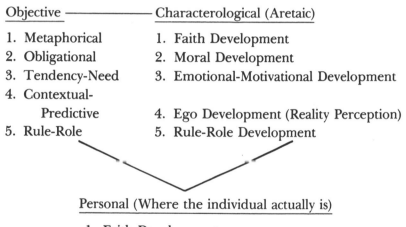

Personal (Where the individual actually is)

1. Faith Development
2. Moral Development
3. Emotional-Motivational Development
4. Ego Development
5. Rule-Role Development

The Metaphorical Level

All thinking rests on a foundation of metaphors. We start thinking about the world in metaphors and symbols long before we start making discrete propositional statements. In fact, our discursive and propositional statements grow out of and assume metaphorical levels of apprehending the world. Paul Ricoeur expressed this truth in his celebrated phrase, "The symbol gives rise to thought."[1] More recently the same point has been made by George Lakoff and Mark Johnson in their *Metaphors We Live By*: "The essence of metaphor is understanding and experiencing one kind of thing in terms of another."[2] To use such expressions as "argument is war" or "time is money" is to think metaphorically about both argumentation and time.

We do this in all aspects of our thinking and conceptual lives, but especially in our religious thinking. When it comes to speaking about the most ultimate (in the sense of most determinative) aspect of our experience, we do it in metaphorical language. None of us knows directly the ultimate context of experience; therefore we take more familiar and tangible aspects of experience and apply them metaphorically to the intangible and mysterious ultimate features of experience.

The metaphors we use to represent the ultimate context of experience function to orient us toward that context, form our expectations, teach us to see the world in a certain way, and give us the basic vision by which we live. Through our metaphors we thus learn to see the world at its foundations as either warm or cold, responsive or indifferent, predictable or capricious, demanding or permissive, for us or against us.

In Christian theology, as H. Richard Niebuhr has pointed out,[3] we have used the metaphors of creator, governor, and redeemer to represent our experience of God as the ultimate and most determinative aspect of experience. Buddhism and some forms of existentialism, on the other hand, have tended to use the metaphors of the void. Even the various sciences have their metaphors of the most determinative context of experience. And insofar as they have been used dogmatically to account *exhaustively* for the most truly determinative aspects of experience, these scientific metaphors function as faithlike statements analogous to the metaphors of creator, governor, and redeemer in Christian theology. We see this happening in some dogmatic and positivistic uses of the metaphors of free variation and natural selection in evolutionary theory, in the mechanistic billiard ball analogies in Newtonian physics, in the hydraulic metaphors found in the early Freud or his later metaphors of "life" and "death" as the ultimate forces controlling biological life, and finally in the more romantic metaphors of harmony and "complementarity of excellences" found in humanistic psychology and free-market economics.[4]

The metaphors of creator, governor, and redeemer applied to God orient the Christian toward a particular vision of the world. This vision colors all that we say and do. It affects our moral thinking. Even though it does not determine it in all respects, it deeply influences the way we regard and care for one another. In affirming God as creator we affirm that creation is good in all of its basic aspects. The Genesis account makes the point with compelling simplicity: "God saw everything that he had made, and behold, it was very good" (1:31). James Gustafson says it well: "From the Creation story in Genesis, from the testimony of the Psalms, and from Jesus' valuation of persons and things . . . , one can affirm that first, each thing is good in its particularity, and secondly, that all things are good in relationship to each other . . . even the sinner is good, and he can be good for others in some way that a righteous man cannot be."[5] Something like this fundamental attitude toward things and persons is probably crucial to our care for one another—and implicit in every genuine helping relationship whether religious or secular.

But this same good God who creates a good world in which to live is also governor and judge. Use of these metaphors as well says two things: (1) that God is a morally serious God, and (2) that although the world was created good, there is still fault, conflict, and sin within it. The governor and judge expects things of us. But just what God expects of us is difficult to discern. Probing that question raises a whole range of other questions about the relation of our religious faith to ethics. So our metaphors drive toward orientation and vision, but also toward inquiry.

And finally, the metaphor of redeemer applied to God suggests that—in spite of fault, conflict, sin, and brokenness—forgiveness and renewal are possible. In fact, within the Christian context God's grace is seen as empowering us to change, to repent, and to recommit ourselves to the grateful and morally serious life. This has meant further that at all times and everywhere, to varying degrees, Christians have assumed that the dynamics of sin and grace are somehow connected with every act of care.

But how does the foundational metaphorical level actually affect our practical moral thinking? It raises a fundamental question in religious ethics and moral philosophy—the question of the relation of religion to morality. Moral philosophy, for instance, furnishes strong arguments for the independence of morality from religion—any religion be it Christianity or some other. Religious people often find such an assertion upsetting, but it need not be if one takes the time to think through the arguments. Plato credits Socrates with having first raised the question when he asked in the *Euthyphro*, "Is something right because God commands it or does God command it because it is right?" In other words, is there such a thing as moral rightness independent of God's command? The argument for the independence of morality from religion is basically this: if God were to command something clearly immoral, like unjustifiably killing someone, the fact that God commands it would not make it right. Conversely, some moral philosophers would argue that we *know* what God commands is morally right only because we have some prior understanding of the moral which is independent of God's command. Thus when Jim Jones tells us that God commanded him to take the lives of the Jonestown colony we know either that Jones is deluded, not telling the truth, or that God is immoral. We know by our own independent judgment that tricking hundreds of people into suicide is immoral, and accordingly we conclude either that Jones's revelation is false or that God is of questionable character. The conclusion of this line of thinking, then, is simply that morality is something independent of religion—independent of God's specific commands, instructions, and laws. It may well be that God reinforces the morally right, conforms to it himself, and even motivates us to be moral. But even if all that is true, one still would need to admit that formal moral judgments retain at least some independence from religion.

This point of view, strongly argued by many moral philosophers especially those of a Kantian persuasion, is accepted even today by some theological ethicists. Such acceptance, however, does not mean that religion makes no difference to our morality. H. Richard Niebuhr, Gustafson, Stanley Hauerwas, Ernest Wallwork, and others have argued convincingly that although, strictly speaking, moral judgments may be logically or formally independent of religion, religion still makes a difference to morality.[6] In short, these theological ethicists argue that our religious metaphors and stories teach us a different vision of the world—teach us to "see" the world differently—and that this difference *makes a difference* to our moral judgments. Whatever our specific moral principles happen to be, they will function differently if our metaphors of ultimacy tell us that we live in a basically warm and providential world with an open future rather than the center of a black hole where all is collapsing and there is no tomorrow, or in a basically hostile world where the fates play fiendish tricks on defenseless mortals. To put it more bluntly, we may not need religion to tell us how to do the formal moral act of dividing a piece of bread equally between four different people, but our understanding of the meaning of the act and *why* we should do it will be greatly affected by the kinds of metaphors of ultimacy (religious understandings) we bring to such a moral act.

This tradition in theological ethics, associated particularly with the names of H. Richard Niebuhr, Gustafson, and Hauerwas, strikes an antiformalist note in our understanding of moral rationality. From their perspective, moral decision making is never just a matter of employing abstract formal principles of obligation, whether Kantian, utilitarian, or ethical egoist. Our formal principles are always surrounded by symbolically mediated visions of the world that make a difference to how we apply our formal principles. Hauerwas summarizes the point:

> We neither are nor should we be formed primarily by the publicly defensible rules we hold, but by the stories and metaphors through which we learn to intend the variety of our existence. Metaphors and stories suggest how we should see and describe the world—that is how we should "look-on" ourselves, others, and the world—in ways that rules taken in themselves do not. Stories and metaphors do this by providing the narrative accounts that give our lives coherence.[7]

Hauerwas argues that religious stories and metaphors are not reducible to formal principles and rules. For instance, the Christian story that depicts God as the father of all human beings (thereby making all humans brothers and sisters in God) and as acting in Christ to redeem his children—such a story cannot be reduced to the abstract principle "to treat others fairly." Hauerwas claims that for the person influenced by this story, human beings "are not just to be treated fairly; they are literally brothers (and sisters) in Christ."[8] Vision, metaphor, and story are nonreducible dimensions of moral thinking and moral decision making.

But if the task of doing practical theology in a pluralistic society is both correlational and critical, how do we compare and evaluate different metaphors and stories about the ultimate context of our experience? How do we compare, evaluate, and assign relative adequacy to the metaphors of God as creator, governor, and redeemer as over against the metaphors of the void, or the Freudian metaphors of life and death, or the mechanistic metaphors dogmatized in some of the sciences, or the metaphors of harmony found in humanistic psychology?

There are two answers to this question, only one of which can be elaborated to any extent in this book. One answer has to do with tests that are basically metaphysical, the other with tests that are basically moral. A metaphysical test asks how our metaphors of ultimacy account for and help explain the various aspects of our experience—namely the cognitive, moral, and aesthetic experiences that are part of our everyday life.

For our purposes a more practical and useful test, however, is the moral test. Moral experience is part of our general experience; it is therefore a dimension of the metaphysical test. But the moral dimension can be factored out for more systematic attention. We can ask, How do our metaphors of ultimacy support and cohere with our moral intuitions and what we know to be morally right? This suggests that our moral principles, although informed by our religious metaphors, are indeed independent of them (as some moral philosophers suggest) and can actually be used to test the adequacy of competing religious views of the world. In fact we make these kinds of judgments all the time. We do it when we say that Jim Jones's view of God as a suspicious and vengeful God is not adequate because it does not cohere with what we otherwise know to be morally right. Or we do it when we say, as William James did, that monistic or pantheistic concepts of God are not fully adequate (which does not mean they are totally inadequate) because they squeeze out the possibilities of agency and freedom needed for moral action.[9]

In his representation of God, Peter Spicer referred to only one of the traditional Christian metaphors—the metaphor of God the redeemer. He made no mention of God the creator or of God the governor, or of what these metaphors might mean for a ministry to Jim and Betty Farr. The love of God in his redemptive activity is Pastor Spicer's only operative religious metaphor in his discussion of the case. From that single metaphor, however, he moves in surprising directions. God's love is invoked on behalf of an ethical-egoist view of personal fulfillment for the Farrs—which at the same time reduces their marriage covenant to a matter of secondary if not nonexistent concern. Aside from the peculiarity of coupling metaphors of God's love with ethical-egoist principles of obligation, one wonders what difference it would have made in the way Pastor Spicer talked about his case had he made more use of the metaphors of God as creator and God as governor. If he had used the metaphor of God as governor, might he have said more about the Farrs' obligations to each other and less about their self-actualization? If he had used the metaphor of God as creator, would this have led him to espouse the historic orders-of-creation arguments or natural-law arguments about the purpose of marriage? How would such metaphors have affected his view of the case and of what he should do?

The Obligational Level

The story that God created the world, made it good, and redeemed it when it fell is relevant and makes a difference, but it does not give us all that we need for addressing the crucial moral issues of our time—abortion, sexuality, homosexuality, economic and racial justice. Gustafson argues that the story of Jesus Christ and our relation to him may make a substantial contribution to our ethical thinking, but from it "comes no single specific inference for the moral life."[10] To it must be added more specific principles, rules, and value judgments for the purpose of guiding and shaping our concrete moral thinking. Some of these may be derivable from the Christian story, but never without difficulty, and never without special effort to examine them for their universal validity. The point is that we have not arrived at the obligational level of moral rationality until we can enunciate more specific moral propositions and ethical maxims. In their theological ethics H. Richard Niebuhr and Hauerwas fail to do this. It is good to state, as they do, that our moral principles always have behind them some metaphorical vision of the world, and that this vision makes a difference. But it is another matter to fail to articulate, as they generally do, moral principles to guide us through the intricacies of moral reflection.

One has arrived at the obligational level of moral rationality (and practical moral theology) only when one can state summarily what one believes to be moral. Kant's categorical imperative—"Act only on that maxim which you can at the same time will to be universal law"—is the kind of principle that puts us at the obligational stage. The Golden Rule ("Do unto others as you would have them do unto you") and the Second Great Commandment ("You shall love your neighbor as yourself") are also statements of moral obligation. Utilitarian and ethical-egoist principles are also examples of what I mean by the obligational level.

Any of these different theories of obligation can be coupled with different metaphorical representations of the ultimate context of reality. For instance, Kant's categorical imperative can be embraced within the context of a Buddhist, existentialist, or Christian understanding of ultimate reality. Yet the way Kant's principle would actually function—whether, for instance, it would entail any interest in the claims of future generations—would be seen quite differently, depending upon which set of metaphors becomes its bracketing context.

The principles of love and justice, for example, are generally seen to be the two great moral principles animating the Judeo-Christian tradition. But what principles of obligation do love and justice imply or in light of what philosophical principles are they to be interpreted? Should they be interpreted teleologically, deontologically, or by some combination of the two?

In my opinion the single most powerful principle of obligation is indeed associated with Kant's categorical imperative—and its important restatement in John Rawls's principle of "impartiality" or "justice as fairness," which has significant analogies with major principles of obligation in both Christianity and Judaism. In *A Theory of Justice* Rawls tries to refine Kant's principle by asking all of us who are involved in ethical conflict and deliberation to imagine ourselves stepping behind a veil of ignorance that would have the effect of blinding us to particular knowledge about ourselves—we are to assume ignorance about how a moral decision would affect us personally. Being thus blind to our own particular interests, we should then design a system that would be fair to ourselves no matter where we started in life, no matter what our particular educational, class, intellectual, and cultural characteristics might be. Rawls believes that when we imaginatively place ourselves in this situation of blindness, our natural capacity for inference and generalization—our natural reasoning capacities—will function to show us what is just and fair.[11]

In short, to reason morally (or to put our reasoning powers at the service of moral ends) is to think reciprocally or reversibly, as Jean Piaget and Lawrence Kohlberg have shown. That is to say, by reason we come to understand that it is unfair to make claims on someone else that we are unwilling for that person to make on us. To think morally is to have and exercise some basic powers for inference and reversibility: if it is not all right for Jack to make this claim on me, then (by reversing the logic) it is not all right for me to make a similar claim on Jack. When we generalize such thinking to include not only

Jack and me but everyone else as well, and do so under the postulated veil of ignorance about our own special interests, then we begin to approach the kind of disinterested impartiality that Rawls believes to be the essence of morality.

Hence, both the Golden Rule and the Second Great Commandment are, in the first instance, invitations *to think*. They are invitations to practical moral rationality. In order to love your neighbor as yourself, or do to others as you would have them do to you, you must be able to think rationally, and especially to think reversibly and impartially. Thus there is at the very heart of the Judeo-Christian tradition a core of practical moral rationality which we frequently fail to understand and appreciate. Furthermore, the style of practical moral rationality found in this tradition, when it is true to itself, can be articulated and even defended philosophically and publicly.

From this perspective it can be argued that there are no special moral principles unique to Christianity. What is special is the belief that whatever is thoroughly moral partakes of the nature of God, and that God in turn supports that which is thoroughly ethical in the best human sense of the term. Ronald Green in his provocative *Religious Reason* has taken this Kant-Rawls tradition directly into religious ethics and used it to interpret the ethical traditions of both ancient Judaism and primitive Christianity.[12] Green believes that in ancient Judaism God was indeed depicted as possessing the characteristics of perfect impartiality outlined in Rawls's theory of justice as fairness. God "is not partial and takes no bribe. He executes justice for the fatherless and the widow, and loves the sojourner, giving him food and clothing" (Deut. 10:17–18). This impartiality, Green tells us, was assigned by the rabbis to both God's justice and God's mercy. God must be seen as exemplifying perfectly the features of moral rationality, the same moral rationality which humans—because of their finitude and sinfulness—exemplify only partially and fragmentarily. Green also sees this kind of impartial moral reason to be fundamental to what both the Golden Rule and the Second Great Commandment are trying to say.

Green gives a highly original interpretation of Pauline theology and its understanding of Jesus Christ as the moral symbol par excellence. By suggesting that in Paul's theology Christ is a moral figure of unusual power, Green is arguing that Christ unifies certain seeming tensions in the moral reason and impartiality of God. Wherein are God's demands contradictory? What tension in God's impartiality does Jesus Christ reconcile? Green believes there is a tension between God's universal and impartial justice on the one hand and God's loving forgiveness and mercy on the other.[13] Ancient Judaism believed that God's forgiveness is real but reaches sinners only after they have themselves first repented. This of course leads to the question, Whence comes the power to repent, especially if the sinner is already overburdened with the weight of paralyzing guilt?

Green points out that although Paul was critical of how the moral law was sometimes used, he was not critical of the intention of the moral law itself or of its central role in the Christian life. As Rom. 1:18–23 indicates, humans (we assume he means normal adults) have a natural capacity to discern the morally right. In addition, Paul seems to assume a correspondence between this natural law and God's revealed law. The law in both senses was, for Paul, like a medical diagnosis; it could tell you what was wrong, but it could not itself provide a cure, the power either to change or to repent. The law can measure, but it cannot transform. Christ, on the other hand, is *the* moral symbol par excellence because through his grace he not only forgives sinners but also transforms and empowers their will. It is this transformation and empowerment that renews the sinner's capacity to pursue the demands of the moral law. The sinner's righteousness comes indeed from God through Jesus Christ: "It is no longer I who live, but Christ who lives in me" (Gal. 2:20). The righteousness of sinners is not their own, but it is nonetheless righteousness—or at least a renewed capacity for righteousness. Although mercy is granted, the law itself is upheld.

We have now abstracted from the Christian story and its metaphors of ultimacy a principle of obligation—reversible impartiality of the kind celebrated in the Golden Rule and in the Second Great Commandment. This principle helps us to understand the metaphor of God as governor and illuminates the moral seriousness of the Judeo-Christian tradition. Moreover, the principle is to be found in analogous formulations in a variety of other metaphorical and religious settings throughout history—further illustration of how moral principles indeed have some independence of their religious metaphorical contexts.

In the Christian context the principle of impartiality is equally fundamental for a proper interpretation of both justice and love (*agape*). In justice there is a more direct emphasis upon impartiality, equality, and reciprocity. In love as *agape* we are called to be more active, more directly empathic, more specifically identified with the unfortunate, more self-sacrificing and aggressive in trying to meet needs and redress inequalities. But we still do this impartially, without regard to the special qualities and values of the other persons and without elevating our own claims above theirs. As Green says, impartiality "can be fused with a profound emotional concern for the other, on the model of family love, so that a moral life based on this virtue must culminate not only in a strict regard for the moral rules, but where morally permissible, in genuine acts and attitudes of supererogation."[14] But because in the Christian religion this principle of moral rationality has as its framework certain basic metaphors about the ultimate context of experience (God as creator, governor, and redeemer) it should be clear why practical moral rationality and practical moral theology are so closely allied.

Peter Spicer should probably have emphasized such justice and love as goals of the human fulfillment he envisioned for Jim and Betty Farr. It might have been truer to the Christian tradition to say that his purpose was to help them learn to handle their own needs (their own self-actualization) *in such a way* as not to make unjust claims on each other and those around them. It might have been a more defensible understanding of fulfillment to see his goal as that of helping them become more *agapic* with each other, more actively open to an impartial concern for each other's needs, not just their own.

If such an understanding of goal and purpose is more defensible both theologically and philosophically, then Pastor Spicer might wish to change his language as well. He might say that his goal, rather than that of fostering individual self-actualization for both Jim and Betty, would be to help them, individually and together, to develop the *power* and *capacity* to live ever more impartially loving lives. And in the process of moving toward that goal, he might indeed be interested in helping them actualize their various needs and potentialities. Clearly, part of their growth could entail coming to understand and serve their own needs better, not as ends in themselves (as the doctrine of self-actualization seems to say) but as an empowerment for relating to others in more just and loving ways. After all, if we are to love our neighbor as ourselves, we must indeed love ourselves, knowing and empathizing with our own needs. If we do not empathically understand our own needs, we lack the requisite tools for empathically and impartially considering the needs of others; we have insufficient tools for pursuing love and justice. Pastor Spicer should probably try to understand the growth he wishes for the Farrs in terms of this theory of obligation. The language of self-actualization would be at best transitional; it would be used to help Jim and Betty address their own needs and actualize their own powers, not as an end in themselves, but as means toward a higher goal of self-transcendence in relating to others.

The Tendency-Need Level

The last three levels of moral rationality can here be reviewed more briefly. The case studies of chapter 7 will allow for illustrating them more fully.

The difficulty with interpreting the Christian obligations of love and justice in terms of the principle of impartiality is that impartiality is such an abstract principle. Impartiality universalized probably gets to the very heart of moral thinking, but like any universal principle, it remains rather formal and empty unless it is supplemented by a generic theory of human nature, by some theory of what the central tendencies and needs of humans really are. Green says as much: "Valid moral reasoning depends not merely upon the willingness to generalize principles but equally upon an impartial standpoint and, from that standpoint, a rational weighting of all the differing needs and desires involved in instances of social conflict."[15] Elsewhere he writes that moral principles are those that "serve the interests, not of one or another particular person, but of men generally, that is, of individuals deprived of all the knowledge that distinguishes them from one another and limited to the knowledge of their general qualities."[16]

Here Green, following Rawls and Kant, is actually putting forth a deontological theory of obligation. It is deontological not only because Green believes abstractly that impartiality is the nature of God, but because, in addition, his theory does not justify moral actions primarily on the basis of the good consequences that follow from them. What makes an act moral is its impartiality, not the specific quantity of nonmoral consequences—the amount of various goods—that flow from it. The reversible moral judgments exemplified in impartiality are moral in and of themselves, without reference to consequences. Green, and probably Rawls and Kant as well, are of course interested in consequences, but the logic of how they work consequences into their theory is different from the standard teleological arguments. Utilitarianism, for example, as a form of teleology appeals directly to consequences: the right rule or act is that which leads to the greatest good for the most people. But there is a problem with this kind of teleology that Green and other deontologists are trying to avoid: rules or acts which lead to the greatest good for the most people can sometimes lead to gross injustice. This possibility is a problem for utilitarian moral philosophers and teleological utilitarians, such as Joseph Fletcher, who explicitly interpret *agape* in terms of consequences. It is possible to increase the overall amount of good—but at a considerable expense to a minority of the people and sometimes a sizable minority at that. The utilitarian should be happy if more good is enjoyed by 75 percent of the people—even if 25 percent are worse off. For utilitarians, justice as fairness is not the first criterion of morality; their first interest is rather the overall increase of good, even if this good is enjoyed by only some of the total population.

Injustice of this sort can, however, be avoided by putting the concern with impartiality ahead of the concern with consequences. This is exactly what the Kant-Rawls-Green perspective accomplishes. But once this formal principle is established—impartiality first!—then a concern for needs and interests (goods and consequences) must, as Green points out, inevitably come back into the picture. The question then becomes, Which of all the various conflicting human tendencies, wants, and needs are now to be justly, fairly, and lovingly—impartially—met? In short, every theory of moral rationality needs also a theory of what our central human tendencies and needs truly are, so that in situations of conflict or scarcity we can decide which ones should be fairly and responsibly met. Green acknowledges that moral rationality needs such information, but he makes no effort to discover it. This failure leaves him, and Kantians like him, with a formalist ethic that is incomplete, insufficient for purposes of making actual moral judgments.

Where then do we get our information about human tendencies and needs? We get them from at least three places: (1) our own intuitive experience, (2) religious and cultural traditions, and (3) the sciences of the human such as psychology, sociobiology, and sociology. We humans have many tendencies, wishes, and wants, not all of which can actually be thought of as legitimate needs in the proper sense of that word. In situations where these tendencies and wishes conflict with one another we are constantly trying to determine which ones are most central and most compatible with a wide range of other nonmoral goods and needs. The catalog of values in Genesis illustrates the way in which religious traditions convey images of nonmoral goods. "You shall have them [plants] for food"; "Be fruitful and multiply"; "It is not good that . . . man should be alone"—all of which are blessed with the benediction "Behold, it was very good."

But as traditions break down and personal experience becomes confused, humans begin to quarrel with one another about what their basic needs really are. This throws them into a comparative mentality whereby they attempt critically to correlate their historically inherited perceptions of value with what the sciences have discovered about the central tendencies of human beings. I agree with the early judgment of James and with the more recent arguments by Mary Midgley,[17] George Pugh,[18] Peter Singer,[19] and Stephen Toulmin that factual information from the sciences about our central human tendencies can inform ethical rationality. This can happen, however, not because one can from these facts logically derive an appropriate theory of moral obligation, but because, once our principle of obligation is established, it in turn receives its content, and transcends its purely formal character, by attempting to mediate between conflicting needs and wants, by discerning those most compatible with one another, and by attempting to realize justly, fairly, and impartially for the community as a whole just those needs that are most basic for human life. We will try to illustrate how this works in the case studies of chapter 7, which show pastoral care and moral discernment working together in situations involving homosexuality.

The Last Two Levels

It is only when the theological thinker moves beyond the metaphorical and obligational levels and gets into the lower levels that practical theology proper occurs. I will only mention the last two levels now, with a view to discussing them more fully in the chapters that follow.

The fourth level of practical moral rationality is the contextual-predictive level. This is the level where we try to interpret the situation that confronts us in our ethical deliberation. Here we try to determine the sociological, psychological, and cultural trends and forces that bear upon the situation. In admitting the need to do this analysis of context, I must follow quickly with a word of caution. Judgments about the forces and trends operating in our context do not determine either the metaphors by which we interpret life (level one) or our principles of obligation (level two). Analysis of our context, however, is important for determining which of the non-moral needs, values, and goods (level three) alluded to above are compatible with one another in a specific time and place and can therefore be justly and impartially protected and enhanced as long as this particular context obtains. Clearly the human sciences—especially psychology and sociology—can here play a crucial role.

At this level of ethical thinking we are indeed interested in consequences. Let it be emphasized once again, however, that concern about consequences does not justify our principles of obligation. But once impartiality has been selected and informs both our love and our justice, then consequences can indeed be a legitimate matter of interest.

And finally at level five, after we have gone through all four preceding steps, we can come up with specific rules and roles for organizing our practical action. At this level, rules may well be variable and changing—indeed, as the situation changes, our rules will need to change—but our higher-level principles of obligation should not change. The fact that our rules may change, however, does not make us situation ethicists or utilitarians. We do not change the rules in order to produce more good for more people; rather we alter the rules in order to bring about a more just distribution of good for everyone in the evolving situation that we confront. Even at this rule-role level, however, it must be observed that our situations do not change as much as we moderns are inclined to think, and that in most instances the rules that have served us well in the past can be presumed to serve us well in the future—unless clearly proven otherwise. The concrete rules and roles of the past should always be accorded the honor of commendable hypotheses that probably had a point at one time and may still have a point today. They are at least candidates for serious reflection and testing.

CHAPTER 7

Two
Case Studies

Bringing dynamic psychological judgments and ethical judgments closer together can improve our care, both religious and secular, but it can also help us achieve a better-integrated culture in which to live. Confusion abounds if the goals of our care—our counseling, psychotherapy, advice giving—seem to be at odds with other cultural norms for human living. In this chapter I will present two case studies—one from a pastor's counseling with a male homosexual and the other an analysis of three denominational statements on homosexuality. They will illustrate some of the points I have been making.

The position I will develop portrays individuals of homosexual orientation as being both human and deserving of justice and full access to all civil and religious privileges. If they wish, they should be fully accredited as members of the Christian church. They are worthy of the church's advocacy. At the same time, however, the church will also want to hold up the image of covenanted heterosexual marriage as the normative pattern for organizing human sexuality. This chapter is dedicated to clarifying these statements.

GOALS IN PASTORAL CARE

Some readers may feel that all our intellectual effort in these chapters till now has accomplished little—except to establish the point that self-actualization should not be the goal of Peter Spicer's work with Jim and Betty Farr. Although this is surely part of the point, my full thesis is more complex and distinctive than that. Love and justice (defined in terms of impartiality) should be the overriding purpose of such pastoral care, though self-actualization can indeed be dialectically related to these more self-transcending goals. Discerning and meeting some of our own needs and actualizing some of our own potentialities may be a partial prerequisite for having the power and empathy to transcend ourselves in love and justice for the other.

This truth is recognized in the commandment "You shall love your neighbor *as yourself.*" Self-love (taking care of one's own needs and actualizing one's own powers) is here acknowledged as a partial presupposition for the possibility of loving the neighbor. Self-love is not the goal, but without some love of self we seem unable to love our neighbor either. Self-love, as the Second Great Commandment articulates it, seems to be a guide to the more self-transcending love of neighbor.

Eros and Agape

In the terminology of more traditional theological discussions, what is involved here is the debate between *agape* and *eros.* These two Greek words refer to two forms of love. *Agape* refers, in terms of our discussion, to impartial love of the other without regard to the particular qualities possessed by the other and what they might do to enhance me. *Eros,* on the other hand, is love of the other precisely for the sake of those qualities and values which the other possesses that might enhance me, that is, help to meet my needs and actualize my powers.

So far as the traditional debate is concerned, I would stand closer to Paul Tillich and Reinhold Niebuhr than to Anders Nygren, who sees *agape* as the true goal of the Christian life and *eros* as making no contribution to *agape.* Tillich and Niebuhr both see *eros* as contributing to *agape,* even though *agape* does transcend the self-regard that is typical of *eros.* Both Niebuhr and, to an even-greater degree, Tillich feel that *eros* contributes positive energies and empowerments to *agape,* whereas *agape* in turn transforms *eros* and fashions its energies to more other-regarding concerns.

But I would make the point even more strongly than either Tillich or Niebuhr: *eros* (my striving to meet my own needs and actualize my own powers) is a positive guide in my efforts to love others. We literally do not know how to assess the fundamental and generic needs of other persons unless we have some access to our own basic needs. Not only is this the testimony of the Second Great Commandment; it is also a strong emphasis in the psychology of Erik

Erikson with its concept of generativity, and in the writings of Heinz Kohut with their beautiful description of empathy.[1] Nonetheless, the theologians are correct in suggesting that unmoderated *eros* (self-actualization) does not automatically engender that true love to which Christians normally refer when they speak of *agape;* some transformation of *eros* is needed.

Hence it is confusing—and both theologically and socially misleading—for Pastor Spicer to speak of self-actualization as the primary goal of his work with Jim and Betty Farr. This is true even though, at a particular level, meeting Jim and Betty's needs for a more consistent and cohesive sense of self could doubtless make a contribution toward their becoming more just and loving people. It could but it might not. It might simply empower them to become more forthrightly egoistic and self-seeking. Everything depends on the context of meanings brought to the pastor's care and counseling with the Farrs. Self-actualization might lead to even more ruthless and uninhibited pursuit of self-interest or it might be transitional to a more genuine self-transcendence in love of the other.

In this respect, Pastor Spicer has a problem. It would be confusing for him to preach about *agape* from the pulpit while using only *eros* as a guide in his acts of care. Yet theologically and socially it would be even more misleading and inadequate for him to hold up *eros,* in both pulpit and care, as the ideal norm. To do that would be to misrepresent the main goal of the Christian life and to set forth a goal of life that could not be defended philosophically and publicly.

The Issue of Homosexuality

But why tackle the knotty problem of homosexuality in a book on pastoral care? Frankly, I do so with hesitation. Like any author, I would like to please and win my readers, and I realize that in discussing the topic of homosexuality there is little likelihood that anything I say will be universally affirmed. In fact, the reverse is more likely to be true: whatever I say may well trigger hostility and rejection on all sides. But in spite of this danger, I am convinced that the issue of homosexuality can be an instructive one, both as a matter for pastoral care and as a problem in ethics.

I do not presume for a moment to be saying the last word on the subject here. Indeed, it is not a subject area where "last words" are appropriate. But it is a topic deserving of calm, careful, loving, unanxious, and undogmatic reflection. On such reflection the topic does yield to analysis—and is a good one for illustrating the relation of practical moral theology to dynamic psychological perspectives in pastoral care.

Three Pastoral Modalities

Our approach to homosexuality, as to any other issue, will vary depending upon which modality of care we find it necessary to employ—pastoral care, pastoral counseling, or pastoral psychotherapy. These three ecclesial modalities of helping can be distinguished from one another by the extent to which we distance ourselves from an explicitly moral stance in our work with people and focus more narrowly on the psychological dynamics involved.

Pastoral care is clearly the most inclusive category of the three. It must necessarily hold together religious, ethical, and psychological perspectives. In our more or less unstructured general work with youth, young married couples, adults, and the aging, pastoral care maintains a close and intimate connection with ethical norms. Where more structured relationships are involved, as in pastoral counseling on a one-to-one basis, we frequently bracket moral issues, at least for certain periods, and appropriately concentrate on the psychological blocks or developmental impediments to personal growth. Specialized pastoral psychotherapy, which is generally long-term and done by trained professionals, is even more distanced—though never completely divorced—from moral perspectives, and even more strictly focused on psychological and developmental conflicts. Knowing which of the three modalities is called for and what kind of helping relationship to structure, knowing how to communicate expectations and how to begin and end a particular phase of the helping process involve technical issues that go to the very heart of what good care is all about.

Religious perspectives are of course a common and ever-present factor in all three of these helping modalities. Especially discernible, either implicitly or explicitly, are the metaphors of God the creator and God the redeemer. This is true in all forms of care, both religious and secular: we affirm the goodness of creation and the possibilities of change, real renewal—or, as Christians might say, redemption. More variable but still never absent is the metaphor of God the governor. How explicitly and forthrightly we should present the moral point of view in our helping relationships depends on our assessment—diagnosis if you will—of the situation confronting us. But because the moral concern is never absent, and indeed must be quite explicit in all general forms of pastoral care, we need to study carefully how to use it. The moral question obviously looms large in any case study involving homosexuality.

THE CASE OF ARTHUR STRAND

A specialized pastoral psychotherapist, whom we shall call Jeffrey Builder, reports the case of Arthur Strand, who visited Pastor Builder in a counseling center located in a large city of the Southeast. After several sessions Arthur openly acknowledged that he had homosexual tendencies. Since the counselor-client relationship had its setting within the context of specialized pastoral psychotherapy, there was, as we said a moment ago, an appropriate distancing from moral issues and a conscious concentration on developmental and dynamic issues. Nonetheless, as will be seen, moral issues are still present.

Arthur was in his mid-thirties. He was a successful and well-liked partner in a large law firm. Nonetheless he felt that his career was not going anywhere. He came to the pastoral psychotherapist because of difficulties he had experienced in making public presentations and in making certain practical decisions. Arthur spent several sessions with Pastor Builder before mentioning his homosexuality. Up until that time, Arthur had had homosexual experiences only with individuals whom he had met in bars—after becoming almost drunk. After such encounters, he would be afflicted with severe pangs of guilt. In addition to his problems with public presentations and homosexuality, Arthur had experienced difficulties in making certain practical business decisions for himself. Once, he had an opportunity to make a profitable business transaction but could not bring himself to make the necessary final determinations.

Arthur had grown up in a small southern community—in a house he described as having very thin walls: "I could hear everything that my parents said and I was afraid that they could hear me." He admitted to having had little privacy, but for the most part he had accepted this as normal. He also accepted as normal the fact of his mother hovering over him all the time to make sure that he dressed adequately and even going so far as to inspect his bowel and urinary productions. Arthur's father, on the other hand, owned a small business, lived his life on a strict routine, and generally provided no model for Arthur to use as a pattern in helping him differentiate himself from his mother. Yet Arthur professed deep love for both his father and his mother. He worried about hurting them, was preoccupied with thoughts about their old age and death, and wondered if life would have meaning for him without them—especially his mother.

Arthur was highly resistive to talking about people; when he did, he seldom referred to persons by name. He said he would never think of dating a woman because it might hurt her if, not liking her, he should withdraw and not call back. He remembered being self-conscious whenever he undressed before other boys back in grade school and high school, fearing that his penis was abnormally small even though his doctor assured him that it was not. Although the structured environment of college led him to develop a few friends on campus, this was only a brief interlude in a basically friendless world. Jeffrey Builder admitted saying to Arthur on one occasion, after hearing about one of Arthur's one-night stands, "Well, at least you related to someone."

The counselor's assessment was that Arthur had had difficulty modulating his psychological separation from his mother. As a child, and even still, Arthur felt almost merged with his mother, having little sense of identity independent of her. This led Arthur to believe that he had unusual powers to hurt her—and, by analogy, all women. In this assessment of Arthur's case the therapist was adopting and using language and concepts from the new psychoanalytic psychology of the self found in the work of Kohut: Arthur's grandiose self (his earliest sense of being a person of power and competence) was so poorly differentiated from his mother that Arthur believed any exercise of his own power, agency, or initiative might have the effect of hurting, maybe even killing, his beloved mother. The model of Arthur's father was not sufficient to show him a way out of this dilemma. Accordingly, Arthur saw women as dangerous to himself, and himself as dangerous to women. Men were not as dangerous but they were sometimes not as warm as women.

Pastor Builder adopted the therapeutic strategy of "mirroring"—responding with steadfast recognition, almost in the sense of the "unconditional positive regard" or "prizing" proclaimed by Carl Rogers. In this highly empathic mirroring and admiring, the therapist hoped Arthur would learn to establish his own primitive sense of self-esteem and a new sense of self-cohesion—the feeling that he could exercise initiative without destroying other people or himself. The therapist also hoped to help Arthur find a way to exist beyond the alternatives of destroying others or himself (suicide). In helping Arthur achieve this, Pastor Builder knew that he would himself at times subtly affirm and support any efforts on the part of Arthur to relate to other people, even if this entailed homosexual encounters. The therapist tended to see the *goals* of therapy in terms of the realistic *possibilities.*

After fifteen months of therapy Jeffrey Builder felt good about the progress they were making together. Arthur Strand had quit drinking and smoking. He had decreased his one-night stands. He had moved into the homosexual community. He was making progress in overcoming his isolation from people. Many of the relationships he was developing now involved a more complex and varied social life. Arthur had begun to hope for a more permanent relationship, one that would involve sex as well as friendship.

At first glance, one might think that there is nothing either religious or ethical about what this pastoral counselor is doing with this client; Pastor Builder's language and self-understanding seem completely psychological in their orientation. But to judge by first glance would be to miss the full fact—the full event—of what is happening in the counselor-client relationship. Much that is happening is both religious and ethical—although from the perspective of our five levels it might be said that the counseling is religiously and ethically incomplete.

First, it is clear that Jeffrey Builder has attitudes toward Arthur Strand that require certain metaphors of ultimacy to explain and justify. In fact, since Jeffrey is a pastoral counselor, we can imagine what these metaphors are. Certainly the metaphors of God the creator and God the redeemer are functioning in the background of his relationship with Arthur. Foundational attitudes about the goodness of creation and the fundamental worth of Arthur Strand permeate the therapeutic encounter.[2] Arthur's wants, fears, needs, subjectivity, fantasies, and irrationalities are taken seriously, prized, attended to. It is as if the therapist were saying, "Amidst all of this confusion and pain there is still goodness and significance. We have here something on which to build, something to go forward with." Arthur's needs for intimacy, interpersonal affirmation, and self-cohesion are taken seriously. The very possibility of the therapist's "mirroring" Arthur with steadfast recognition presupposes Pastor Builder's belief that Arthur is a person of infinite worth and value—someone made in the image of God and valued by the most fundamental Power in the universe. To ground Jeffrey Builder's attitudes of acceptance and affirmation we are forced—as Thomas C. Oden and I argued years ago and David Tracy and Stephen Toulmin have argued more recently but for different purposes—to seek out a "limit language."[3] Religion provides this limit language. In the Judeo-Christian tradition the metaphors about the goodness of creation provide it for Jeffrey Builder.

But Pastor Builder requires other metaphors as well, metaphors to ground his belief and hope that Arthur Strand can change, grow, improve—however one might phrase it. Might the metaphors of God the redeemer provide such grounding? Well, that depends— on the context of interpretation into which Jeffrey Builder as pastoral psychotherapist places Arthur's difficulties. Are they, in Pastor Builder's view, a matter of sin, sickness, problems of living, or what? The particular context of interpretation is determinative. Jeffrey Builder's expectations and hopes at least are clearly grounded on certain visions and metaphors about the world which say that change and renewal are possible.

What if Jeffrey Builder were not a pastoral counselor, however, but a secular psychotherapist? After all, at one level he clearly is using the interpretative framework of psychoanalytic theory used by many secular therapists. Yet even a secular therapist, if pushed, would still doubtless resort here to metaphorical language of some kind (not necessarily Christian) to express the basic beliefs which lead him to affirm the world and the personhood and needs of Arthur Strand, and to have hope for Arthur's future. At this level, even the secular therapist operates with some kind of faith, the logic of which is not that much different from the faith of the religious counselor. So the question is not, What makes the pastoral counselor religious? Both the pastoral counselor and the so-called secular counselor are equally religious. The question is, rather, whether the pastoral counselor is truly Christian as his title suggests. And if the secular counselor is not Christian (or Judeo-Christian), what religion undergirds his clearly manifest faith?

As a pastoral counselor, however, Jeffrey Builder does not have recourse only to the metaphors of God as creator and God as redeemer. The metaphor of God as governor can also be dimly detected. Far in the background there seems to be a more diffuse but nonetheless discernible trace of moral seriousness. This pastoral psychotherapist feels obligated to keep Arthur from committing suicide. He seems to believe that for Arthur *some* capacity for relatedness is better than none—even if that relatedness entails homosexual involvements. Pastor Builder seems to nourish the hope that Arthur will achieve more mutual, reciprocal, and steadfast friendships. Is this just a rather lazy, implicit and inadequate moral norm? Is counselor Builder in substance advocating the development of more just and less-exploitative relationships for Arthur? Maybe so. Indeed, it seems as if Jeffrey Builder lives in a moral universe that the metaphor of God as governor would probably symbolize. Furthermore, Pastor Builder's therapy clearly is governed by certain principles of obligation; just which principles they are of course is less clear. In terms of our five-level scheme of practical moral thinking this pastoral counselor is clearly making judgments about levels three and four. He may not be attending to all of Arthur's tendencies and needs (level three), but he does acknowledge and attend to some—especially Arthur's need for a cohesive self. Is this Arthur's only need? Obviously not. He has other needs—as do all of us—for food, shelter, exercise, and much more. As counselor, however, Jeffrey Builder sees this particular need as crucial and foundational if Arthur is ever to learn to handle a wide range of other life tasks. In a broader and more inclusive situation of pastoral care the minister might have had to take account of Arthur's various needs, balance them against the need for cohesion, and possibly guide his care by making moral judgments about how Arthur's needs can be reconciled and balanced with those of the larger community.

At level four, the contextual-predictive level, Jeffrey Builder makes few contextual judgments of a sociological kind—judgments that in the broader situation of pastoral care would be an impossible luxury. He does, however, make some contextual judgments of a psychological kind that have the logic of predictions. On the basis of his psychological assessment (diagnosis) the therapist concludes that Arthur's problems are basically preoedipal, that they have to do primarily with self-cohesion, that they are serious, that self-destruction is a possibility, and that growth in the client's capacity for relationships with anyone, male or female, will be slow. In limiting his contextual judgments primarily to the psychological sphere, Pastor Builder is setting aside a whole range of other contextual judgments of a sociological and cultural kind which the full task of practical moral thinking could not afford to ignore.

Finally, Arthur Strand's therapist even makes judgments, generally implicit, about rules and roles. On the surface, these are few. Pastor Builder seems to be bound by no rules about sexuality—about whether or not sexual exchange is exclusively for those who are married, about whether it is open to members of the same sex or the opposite sex or both. But this first-glance judgment is again superficial. When in response to Arthur's confession of his one-night homosexual encounters the therapist said, "Well, at least you related to someone," Pastor Builder was stating some convictions about certain rules and roles. He was saying that it is better for sex not to be casual and anonymous. He was saying that it is better in one's sexual encounters not to play the role of the drunken, unconscious, remorseful individual who is trying to find intimacy and gratification in connection with self-obliteration. Indeed, his response communicated the judgment that for Arthur even this "relating to someone" was something of a risk. In effect the counselor was saying, "I really wouldn't advocate this, but I acknowledge what you were trying to accomplish." Hence, even at this fifth and lowest level of practical moral thinking, we see Jeffrey Builder the pastoral psychotherapist doing practical moral thinking in the very midst of his therapeutic administrations.

Thus even in a therapy that appears on the surface to use neither religious nor moral language, Pastor Builder the therapist is in fact both religious and moral through and through. Indeed, the situation would not have been noticeably different in principle had he instead been a secular counselor reporting a case. The counseling as such is religious and moral in a certain way and with reference to certain ends. Jeffrey Builder's goals are primarily therapeutic, primarily designed to increase Arthur's sense of selfhood so that he can take more responsibility for himself, make better decisions, love more effectively. The principles of obligation and the rules that would govern the definitions of this heightened responsibility are discernible in the counseling, however vague. The counselor's moral thinking is incomplete but nonetheless present. We may not agree as to the specifics of his moral thinking and judgment, but that is not the point. It is still there; his counseling is not morally neutral—it is not amoral.

Is it possible, however, for the counselor to do a better and more systematic job of moral thinking, even about an issue as challenging as homosexuality, and still relate helpfully to a client such as Arthur Strand? For make no mistake about it: Jeffrey Builder *is* leading

Arthur into some kind of moral world, even if we do not know precisely the moral contours of that world. Such covert moral directedness is a problem for the secular therapist. It can be even more of a problem for the minister, the pastoral counselor, and even the pastoral psychotherapist. Are there ways of making our moral world clearer without sacrificing therapeutic goals and growth-producing change?

DENOMINATIONAL THINKING
ON HOMOSEXUALITY

How would the five-level system of practical moral rationality outlined in chapter 6 relate to the issue of homosexuality? We saw in the case of Jeffrey Builder's counseling that the five levels were actually present and discernible, however incomplete and vague. But how would they look and operate if they were applied more self-consciously and rigorously?

In an effort to illustrate this, I will analyze three studies on the subject of homosexuality. The three are probably illustrative of the practical moral thinking being done in the mainline Protestant denominations of the United States. After analyzing the kind of thinking reflected in these studies, I will present my own constructive alternative based on the method I have here been developing. My discussion of the three studies in the present context will necessarily be condensed. Readers wanting a more leisurely discussion may wish to consult my larger treatment entitled "Homosexuality, Theology, the Social Sciences, and the Church."[4]

The Christian Church (Disciples of Christ) in 1977 issued "A Study Document on Homosexuality and the Church."[5] The United Church of Christ called its 1977 document *Human Sexuality: A Preliminary Study.*[6] The 1978 United Presbyterian Church study, *The Church and the Homosexual,*[7] contains both a minority and majority report. These three studies—excluding the Presbyterian minority report—have astonishing similarities. They all take a modern scholarly critical view of the Bible. They all try to come to terms with information from the human sciences—psychology, biology, and sociology—on homosexuality. And they all take a tolerant and basically approving attitude toward at least some forms of homosexuality. My discussion of these three studies follows the five levels of practical moral rationality set forth in chapter 6.

Metaphors

At the metaphorical level all three studies use God the redeemer as their lead metaphor for representing the ultimate context of human experience. Little reference is made to God the creator or God the governor. Connected perhaps with the disinterest in the metaphor of God the creator is the tendency to repudiate certain classical styles of moral reflection, such as the natural-law argumentation employed in Catholicism or the orders-of-creation argumentation found in Reformation Protestantism. This modern neglect of Catholic natural law is not surprising, but such systematic disregard for the classic Protestant orders of creation is surprising, and we will focus more fully on it later in our analysis.

Obligations

At the obligational level the three studies agree completely on making neighbor love the single moral principle for ordering all of human sexuality. Their common tone is reflected in a few lines from the UCC document: " 'God is love' is the central affirmation of biblical faith that forms the context in which all scripture must be interpreted," and (as regards Jesus' teaching on sexuality), "It is clear that he emphasized the primacy of neighbor love in making moral and ethical decisions."[8]

This neighbor love through which the love of God is expressed is understood deontologically in the sense that God commands it and we do it out of faith and loyalty. But it is also teleological because, in a secondary sense, what God commands has good consequences: it is good for us, if not immediately, at least eventually.[9] The UCC statement is typical: "The basic criterion for judging the worth of attitudes and actions in the Christian community is 'the glorious gospel,' which . . . means the love of God shown in Christ and the welfare and good of all persons in the quest for fullness of life."[10] Such sentiments, liberally expressed throughout the Presbyterian and Disciples studies as well, suggest that we know God's love in the consequences that ensue. Thus all the studies espouse a directly teleological, and probably utilitarian, theory of obligation. Furthermore, this theory of obligation is act-oriented because what is everywhere affirmed is the specific act leading to the best consequences in the unique situation.

Finally, this mixed theory of obligation—deontological and act-utilitarian—functions, as we observed a moment ago, without support from either Protestant orders-of-creation argumentation or Catholic natural-law argumentation. The Presbyterian study raises the question, What do Christians do with Old Testament law and with Israelite orders of creation in light of both Jesus Christ and expanding empirical knowledge?[11] Its answer runs as follows: The Old Testament condemnations of homosexuality reflect the biases of an ancient patriarchal society, and Jewish concepts of the order of creation which specify the primordiality of maleness and femaleness are clearly contradicted by contemporary studies of gender and sex-role identity—"Gender identity and gender role are not biologically fixed categories . . . we humans are free from domination by biologically coded instinctual behavior. As a result of this God-given freedom, we humans share in the creative responsibility for determining what it means to be male and what it means to be female."[12]

No constraints on our patterns of sexual expression are dictated by our human nature, which is plastic, infinitely flexible, and unbounded. Sexuality therefore can take an infinite variety of forms as long as it is consistent with the principle of self-giving love. Arguments about the limits of human nature, whether from orders-of-creation thinking or from natural-law thinking, play no role.

Tendencies and Needs

At the tendency-need level of practical moral reasoning the authority of the human sciences reigns supreme in all three studies. The documents make little effort to correlate ancient insights with those of modern science. Where the human sciences and the ancient traditions conflict, the former already have the greater authority; the traditional sources are assumed to be ethnocentric and culture-bound. All three of the denominational documents accept and affirm the studies by Money, Hampson, and others which seem to suggest that gender identity (whether we think of ourselves as male or female) and sex-role identity (whether we see ourselves as playing a male role or a female role, a passive role or an active role) are basically matters of learning and cultural conditioning. This point of view, which corresponds closely to certain classical psychoanalytic positions, sees human sexuality as highly plastic and nonspecific with regard to aim and object: humans are sexually interested and seek sexual release, but our sexuality is not innately patterned toward either male or female objects and only gradually, under the impact of socialization, does it become oriented one way or the other. Hence, according to this view, we have tendencies and needs to have sex, but no tendencies or innate needs to have it with persons of a specific gender. It is important to observe—and we will return to this later—that all three studies make no effort to survey any of our other basic human needs and tendencies or to determine where our sexual needs fit in the total spectrum of human needs.

Context and Prediction

Because all three studies pay a great deal of attention to the human sciences, they are loaded with information on the contextual level of analysis. In addition, they are full of efforts to make predictions about the consequences of various sexual arrangements. Two of the three make important use of research by Evelyn Hooker which suggests that about the same range of neurosis and health is found among homosexuals as among heterosexuals.[13] All of them take the position—still the dominant position in the human sciences despite certain recent minority reports[14]—that homosexuality is learned and not an innate biological condition. Furthermore, all of them accept the standard human science tradition of distinguishing between homosexual acts and homosexual orientation: a homosexual orientation is a pervasive preference for intimacy with persons of the same sex due to very early experience, learnings, or dynamic interactions, but not all homosexual acts are due to a pervasive orientation. Furthermore, the Disciples and UCC point out that most societies in previous eras have accepted homosexuality far more readily than our Western-Judeo-Christian societies. The UCC study makes this point most emphatically with the questionable argument that "the majority of societies that have been studied have condoned homosexual behavior."[15] Finally, all the studies accept the common human science belief that homosexuality is extremely resistant to psychotherapy unless there is a strong—and rare—motivation to change.

Rules and Roles

At the fifth and last level, what kind of specific rules and roles pertaining to homosexuality do these studies recommend? Much of their effort at this level has to do with biblical interpretation. On the whole they see the Old and New Testament passages commonly cited in this connection not as condemnations or disparagements of homosexuality but instead as expressions of Jewish-Christian ethnocentricity and patriarchalism that are no longer binding.

The practical result for all three studies is that all condemnations of homosexuality, all tendencies to see homosexuality as sinful, and all ecclesial and civil restrictions against the homosexual should be dropped. Homosexuals should be accepted and openly affirmed as individuals. They should enjoy all civil and ecclesial rights. As potentially creative and responsible as anyone else, they should be treated simply as persons having a sexual orientation that is different—one that they did not themselves choose but with which they must live. With these practical rules, with these endorsements of a full and equal role for homosexuals in all aspects of society, I am in hearty agreement.

But at this rule-role level the three studies go even further. The UCC study appears to make homosexuality a coequal pattern of sexual organization on a par with covenanted heterosexual marriage.[16] The Disciples study relativizes marital sexuality by referring to the passage about there being no maleness and femaleness in heaven; Mark 12:18–25 is interpreted to mean that Gen. 1:27–31 and 2:18–25 (about God's creation of man as "male and female" and the "one flesh" nature of their union) has no normative significance for life in the kingdom of God.[17] And the Presbyterian document, while affirming the importance of the Genesis pattern of human sexuality, argues that the centrality of that pattern does not mean that "God intended to limit the possibility for loving companionship and partnership to heterosexual marriages."[18]

Conclusion

In concluding this analysis of denominational thinking on this subject, we should observe how these three studies constitute an extremely interesting and instructive example of the way so much of contemporary biblical hermeneutics functions. One can see just how much of the Bible is affirmed and how much of it is respectfully rejected or set aside, and just where and how the division between the two is made.

Some of the higher-level metaphors (God as love) are used, but others (God as creator and governor) are neglected. Neighbor love as a principle of obligation is affirmed, but on the whole it is disconnected from principles of justice and unsupported by understandings of human nature (human tendencies and needs) as articu-lated in the arguments either from orders of creation or from natural law. A great deal of attention is given to our contemporary social context. And finally, at the lowest levels (involving the most practical moral rules and social roles), biblical patterns are dispensed with altogether and new ones are introduced in their place.

In its general outlines, this procedure is probably justified and faithful. But if at any of the five levels the judgments are wrong—and they frequently are—problems can develop. This is what has happened in the case of these studies.

A CONSTRUCTIVE ALTERNATIVE

The position on homosexuality now to be set forth is an alternative to the one presented in these three denominational studies. Before concluding the chapter I will try to suggest what this constructive alternative might mean for the case of Arthur Strand and Jeffrey Builder.

Shaping an Environment

In spite of the admirable job that all three studies do in presenting the theological reasons for granting full civil and ecclesial respect to people of homosexual orientation, they fail to state just what pattern of sexuality the church most clearly supports. In the Presbyterian study this failure was picked up by the minority report: "Our beliefs about homosexuality thus become paramount in importance. Do we value it, disvalue it, or find it morally neutral? Do we shape an environment that encourages free movement toward homosexual-ity, or one that nurtures heterosexual becoming?"[19] The authors of the minority report develop an alternative position based on the classic Protestant concept of orders of creation, but they give it a novel interpretation.

In fact, the entire metaphor of God the creator is given greater emphasis in their study. In addition, creation itself is given some determinate content: creation is not only good, but also has some basic structures that must be discerned and acknowledged. But in making this point, these authors do not equate creation with biologi-cal or natural creation and, unlike most of the three studies, they do not equate orders-of-creation arguments with natural-law argu-ments. In their view the orders of creation are not natural or biologi-cal structures; they are the patterns God intends for humans as they go about organizing their natural creatureliness. From the perspective of the minority report, the concept of orders, although building on and making a place for certain natural inclinations, is primarily a cultural or transcultural concept designed to bring competing and sometimes disorganized natural tendencies into compatible and mutually supportive organizing structures within the constraints of various environments: "Human life is held in coherence, saved from collapse and chaos by the orders of marriage, family, and society—which are structures maintained by our belief and divine grace. . . . The orders of life are configurations requiring energetic commitment to sustain."[20] These orders are synergistic structures or configurations. Although willed by God, they are not simply arbitrary; they build on our natural human tendencies and organize them, but give them a form which the instinctual tendencies themselves may not dictate in every detail.

Hence, the minority report, although affirmative toward full civil and ecclesial membership and respect for homosexuals, does pull back from affirming homosexuality as coequal to covenanted heterosexuality. In addition, it maintains that ordination should be withheld from self-affirming homosexuals—although possibly not from homosexuals who, remaining celibate, are not evangelical in promoting homosexual values. In this way the authors see the church as maintaining beliefs and shaping an environment which, although pastorally supportive of individual homosexuals, does not sanction, promote, or unwittingly help create pathways of easy access to homosexuality.

This minority Presbyterian report, clearly influenced by classic themes in the Protestant theological tradition (and especially by Helmut Thielicke's *The Ethics of Sex*),[21] comes across as a very confessional and uncritical document. Its basic position deserves a more critical and public defense.

A Functionalist Approach

I would myself share its position but give a more functionalist articulation to its concept of orders of creation. In this concept we have ideas and statements that can serve at the rule-role level to order our conflicting tendencies and needs in morally responsible ways that are also consistent with the possibilities of certain social and cultural contexts. From this perspective I would argue that we should see traditional rules and patterns for the organization of everyday life as hypotheses to be taken seriously. They have the status of recommendations that invite critical reflection. If in the course of such serious consideration we cannot find sufficient critical reasons to maintain them, then we can indeed search for new rules and better patterns.

In an effort to state this more functionalist view with power and succinctness, I will relate it in formula-like fashion to our five levels of practical moral thinking:

> General principles of obligation (level two), nurtured and qualified by metaphors of ultimacy (level one), attempt to mediate lovingly and justly—impartially—between conflicting human tendencies and needs (level three), while taking into account the realistic possibilities and constraints of various social, psychological, and cultural environments or ecological niches (level four). When judgments at these four levels have been made, it should be possible to arrive at rules and roles governing specific actions (level five).

This should make clear the great number of ways in which I disagree with the three denominational studies. They use only the metaphor of God the redeemer (the God of love); I would want to use the metaphors of God the creator and God the governor as well. They are all committed to a mixed deontological and act-utilitarian principle of obligation; I would want a more thoroughly deontological position which interprets both love and justice in terms of impartiality and fairness while still serving human interests and needs. They speak of only one human tendency or need—the tendency toward sexual release without regard to the gender of the sexual partner; I would speak, and will speak presently, of a wide range of human tendencies and needs which must be balanced and justly coordinated. And there are other important differences between us at the contextual-predictive and rule-role levels which I must discuss more fully below. But before moving to these last two levels let me elaborate more fully the differences at level three.

The Plasticity of Human Nature

The three studies emphasize the plasticity of human nature (especially our sexual nature). I would take that principle as seriously but in a different direction. They all suggest that because the newborn has no innate gender identity or sexual preference, therefore no specific gender orientation in sexuality should be expected of any human being. This implies that parental, familial, and societal expectations with respect to sexual preference should be dropped and all humans be permitted to find their own way. Clearly, however, this idea of plasticity in human sexuality can be used to make a quite different point: because of our sexual malleability, the direction cultures give to our sexuality is determined by the need to balance our sexual tendencies with the whole range of other vital human tendencies and needs. Indeed, it is precisely because our sexual nature can go easily in a variety of directions for expression—toward homosexuality, bisexuality, or heterosexuality—that culture helps to shape it for us in certain ways. Historically, the ways in which culture has shaped sexuality have been designed to adjust our sexual tendencies and needs harmoniously with other vital—and sometimes even conflicting—tendencies and needs.

Anthropological Considerations

I will expand the argument. None of the three denominational studies looked at ethnological and anthropological evidence concerning human sexuality. But some consideration of the sexual behavior of the other higher primates is surely relevant to the discussion, and there we find evidence from the animal kingdom consistent with the general view of sexual plasticity for humans. For instance, we know that among apes and monkeys diffuse homosexual and bisexual play is widespread; on the other hand, exclusive homosexuality is rare and generally reflects conditions of unusual deprivation or crowding.[22] Human beings are similar to the other higher primates in this respect, though our sexuality may be even more complicated. We are primates but we are more—we are also creatures of language and intelligence who have a great capacity for toolmaking, mobility, imagination, and creativity. All our basic biological tendencies and needs (and they are doubtless many) are plastic, and for this reason can be made greater and more complex by our linguistic and imaginal capacities. In addition, humans are even more susceptible to and conditioned by learning than the other primates. Although other animals seldom learn exclusive homosexual orientation, humans frequently do.

But it may be that for apes and monkeys, who normally spend their lives roaming in small herds over limited geographical areas, their diffuse homosexual and bisexual play does not disturb or interrupt other vital tendencies and needs—for example, to provide a consistent and predictable environment for the raising of the young. But in the course of evolution, as human transcendence and creativity led to specialization of labor and to more complex living arrangements in towns and cities, the easy harmony enjoyed by the other primates may no longer have been possible for humans. Diffuse homosexual and bisexual activity may increasingly have been experienced as a threat to the stability of other vital values. Heterosexual and covenanted marriage may have emerged as the preferred method for patterning sexuality precisely because it managed to organize and actualize justly a wider range of potentially conflicting tendencies and needs (nonmoral goods).

Organizing Human Needs

What are some of the human needs and tendencies organized by the various sexual patterns and institutions? Casual homosexual relations, for instance, do actualize some human tendencies and needs. They convey pleasure. They provide fleeting moments of interpersonal recognition. But they do little else. Stable, long-term homosexual relationships probably organize a wider range of human tendencies and needs. They meet tendencies toward sexual pleasure, provide security, grant a measure of mutual face-to-face recognition, give the partners that sense of consistent identity which comes with a long-term relationship, and help to bind the couple into a cooperative unit which itself addresses a wide range of other practical tasks in living. If one were to consult psychoanalytic theory, George Pugh's *The Biological Origin of Human Values,* Mary Midgley's *Beast and Man,* and the writings of Erik Erikson, one could amass evidence about the role and place of all these tendencies and needs in human life. Insofar as a homosexual relationship serves such tendencies and needs, it must be seen as a very human institution.

But the covenanted heterosexual organization of sexuality does these things and more. It affords the values of simultaneous sexual pleasure, mutual face-to-face recognition, security, long-term companionship and the consistency of identity to which it contributes, and mutual practical helpfulness with the wider tasks of life. Furthermore, it can combine these values with certain intergenerational values. Heterosexual marriage organizes sexuality in ways that are compatible with having children and providing them with the stable and consistent environment needed to support the long years in which human offspring must be relatively dependent upon adults.

Of course, children not only help assure the survival of the race; they also afford certain intrinsic values to parents. They afford a lifelong source of face-to-face recognition with the younger generation (which Erikson and others believe is an abiding need of middle-aged and older adults).[23] They become an immediate object for exercising "generativity" or expressing our deep-seated—and probably biologically based—need to make a contribution to succeeding generations.[24] And finally, children are intergenerational sources of mutual aid and assistance. All these tendencies and needs too, if time permitted, could be shown to be deeply rooted and pervasive in human beings. Psychoanalytic theory, Pugh, Midgley, Erikson, and many other authors could help us to clarify and authenticate the reality of these tendencies and needs. Hence, heterosexual marriage realizes a higher level of value for its participants than do other methods of organizing human sexuality, and it does so within an institution that can be generalized as a universal way of organizing our sexual impulses.

The Moral Question of Universality

This leads us back to levels one and two. Because the Judeo-Christian tradition has always affirmed the goodness of creation (through the metaphor of God the creator), it has also affirmed those tendencies and needs that seemed to be a part of the generically human; accordingly it should be able to acknowledge some of the real values provided—some of the real tendencies and needs met—by more committed long-term homosexual relationships. Clearly this tradition has also had at the same time a real sense of the limitations—and fallenness—of life. It has realized that some of our human tendencies and needs conflict with one another, especially as situations vary. Some are therefore more central than others, some more basic than others, and some more compatible with others. This is why they must be organized morally. And the most moral order is that which impartially actualizes (love) and impartially adjudicates (justice)—the organization that can be universalized and generalized in precisely this sense. It is clear that neither casual nor long-term homosexual relations can be universalized in this sense. Casual relations exclude and destroy a wide range of legitimate human needs in the name of transient pleasure and recognition. More permanent homosexual relationships cannot be generalized either (although they contain many human features), because if they were, not only would children not be born, but a wide range of intergenerational needs would not be met. This would be true even if the adoption of children by homosexuals were to be socially sanctioned. For a variety of reasons, not least of which would be the mounting shortage of adoptive children, this would be nothing more than an ad hoc accommodation.

The argument developed here represents a functionalist defense of covenanted heterosexual marriage as an order of creation and as the normative organization of sexuality advocated by the church. This does not mean that other organizations of sexuality are not to be tolerated; it means they are not to be advocated. The basic symbols, rituals, energies, and practical rules of the church should, as in the past, be put to the service of covenanted heterosexuality. Homosexuality, especially for persons of homosexual orientation, should not be considered sinful, but neither should it be given coequal status with covenanted heterosexuality.

The Contextual Question

The whole notion that homosexuality can be coequal with heterosexuality is based on the supposition that only those who undergo certain early dynamic learnings or only those who are genetically so endowed will have a homosexual orientation. But the logic of this position is not clear. If, as the human scientists argue, our sexuality is not already preprogrammed at birth, then we become heterosexual only because culture forms us in this way. But if culture were to become completely neutral, divesting itself of preferential symbols and of initiatory rituals that push us one way rather than another, we can assume that our natural tendencies would lead us toward diffuse bisexuality. Although such a society would probably not end up monolithically homosexual, it could easily end up diffusely bisexual—a condition that, from an evolutionary perspective, has long since been seen as incompatible with a wide range of other human tendencies and needs. Hence, covenanted heterosexual relations may justifiably be seen as an order of creation and an intention of God *for humans in complex societies*—not so much to order humans as animals but to order humans whose primate nature is complicated by self-transcendence, imagination, mobility, and intelligence. But it does follow from this position that in some contextual situation radically different from the one here described, we could imagine God's intention—and the best of human moral reason—as sanctioning a slightly different organization of our sexuality. This might be true even though our metaphors of ultimacy and our principles of obligation remained the same.

At level four, the level of context, the three denominational studies made at least two assumptions that need to be reconsidered. One is that the rate of homosexuality has not changed and, therefore, probably will not change. It is true that the rate has not changed. But, as mentioned above, if gender identity and sex preference is something learned, not biologically preestablished, then sexual patterns can change. The way a society is organized can make a difference. And although there is little likelihood that a society will become predominantly homosexual in orientation, it is entirely possible that a society will expand greatly the range of sexual experimentation in general, including homosexual experimentation and bisexual activity in particular. Such softening and blurring of the boundaries of sexual activity would offer little benefit to other basic human needs. Indeed, it would certainly exacerbate the already deteriorated condition of the basic environment provided today for the raising of children.

The second assumption, found especially in the UCC study, is that other societies outside the influence of the Judeo-Christian tradition have in fact accepted and even approved homosexuality. Now, there may well be varying degrees of tolerance in different societies, but it is not true that most other societies have affirmed or sanctioned homosexuality. Marvin K. Opler, after extensive study of this issue, says: "No society, save perhaps ancient Greece, pre-Meiji Japan, certain top echelons in Nazi Germany, and the scattered examples of such special status groups as the berdaches, Nata slaves, and one category of Churkchee shamans, has lent sanction in any real sense to homosexuality."[25]

At the contextual level the major defect of the three denominational studies is their failure to recognize what urbanization and modernization have done to destabilize the kind of sexual commitment that is necessary for the socialization of children. Humans are creative and self-transcending creatures; they create complex structures and societies. But today humans are having a difficult time raising individuals with the requisite emotional security and maturity to handle the complex environment in which they must live. For this reason the church must be clear as to its basic commitments if it hopes to help shape the world in which people live, and help form the people who will have the faith and strength needed to live in that world. The fostering of diffuse sexual commitments, in whatever way, can further destabilize an already-complex environment.

PRACTICAL MORAL THINKING
AND PASTORAL CARE

We have come a long and circuitous way since we last considered the case of Arthur Strand and Jeffrey Builder—which further proves, I suppose, that practical moral thinking is not simple but complex. My goal in this chapter has not been to argue a position that no one can question. My goal has rather been to illustrate a method which I believe is essentially correct. If my conclusions are wrong the reader ought to show where the mistake was made, but such correction is likely to be done, if at all, in terms of my model, and this I think is further confirmation of its basic usefulness.

From one standpoint the method here espoused represents a kind of revised natural-law approach to moral thinking. Rather than assuming that nature actually dictates the direction of morality, however, it tries to order conflicting natural needs and tendencies within the context of different situations. Clearly, in doing this, some knowledge of our natural needs and tendencies—gained either intuitively or from tradition or through the human sciences—is required. Moreover, the mind's natural ability to generalize is called upon in order to establish the universal and impartial point of view that can mediate between these needs and tendencies.

The reader may object that no pastoral psychotherapist—or for that matter no minister in any form of care and counseling—can lay such a heavy reflective load on the people coming for help. That of course is true: no minister should! Our discussion here has been designed rather to help establish the frameworks within which pastoral care can and should function.

But even here the problem of moralism can intrude, and does so in a variety of ways. People can feel that it is moralistic when supposedly divine laws are laid on them in insensitive and uncaring ways. It can also be experienced as moralistic when complex moral defenses and explanations are presented which the person seeking help cannot understand and finds to be dry, rationalistic, and remote. Even though defending moral positions with public reasons is the first step toward getting beyond moralism as authoritarianism, such defense may still be experienced as moralism if the person being helped does not have the emotional freedom to relate to the reasons being articulated.

If moralism is such an ever-present danger, then how is the capacity for practical moral rationality—how is practical theology—useful to Jeffrey Builder as a pastoral psychotherapist? Indeed, how is it useful to the larger task of pastoral care? I will discuss the second of these questions in the next chapter. At this point I will only list several ways in which practical moral thinking is important even for the more-specialized context.

Establishing a Value Context

Practical moral reasoning is essential for establishing the value context of any counseling relationship. Indeed, it is doubly important for the pastoral psychotherapist.

People who seek out a pastoral psychotherapist usually do so because they want—and feel they can count on—certain value commitments in the counselor or therapist of their choice. Furthermore, pastoral psychotherapists have an obligation to be able to affirm in some public way their continuity with the value commitments—both moral and nonmoral—of the wider church.

But what is this value context to be? This is the question that is presently confronting both the church and the larger society. Hence, the pastoral psychotherapist must consciously be a part of this larger task of moral inquiry—this larger general task of practical theology. It is important for Jeffrey Builder to be able to indicate in some public way what his general attitude toward homosexuality is, just as it is important for Peter Spicer to be able to represent his view of marriage. This is true even though both pastors, within the confines of an intimate counseling relationship, may for a time set aside this declarative mood.

But, as we saw in the case of Jeffrey Builder, pastors are inevitably leading their clients somewhere, even if only by silently drawing certain boundaries and eliminating certain options. But what are those values and boundaries, and how does the pastor arrive at them? This is a question that both the pastoral minister and the pastoral psychotherapist should be able to answer—and to answer more adequately than the secular therapist.

Improving Understanding

Practical moral thinking is important for all forms of pastoral care because it helps us gain a clearer idea of what is actually happening at any given time and in any given situation. It improves understanding.

We saw earlier how the five-stage model of practical moral reasoning helped us order the relationship between Jeffrey Builder and Arthur Strand. It helped us to see the religious assumptions undergirding the therapist's attitude. We discerned a fairly general theory of obligation operative in the relationship and commitment on the part of the therapist to meet certain of Arthur's needs—primarily his needs for mirroring and for a cohesive self. It helped us to understand that, even though on the surface the therapist seemed to be neutral or casual about concrete rules relating to homosexuality, the counseling being offered was nonetheless a moral process through and through. But it was a moral process of a certain kind—one designed also to be consistent with the primary task of restoring Arthur's sense of self-cohesion. The higher levels of moral reasoning were to some degree stable and in order; it was only the lower levels that were set aside, bracketed, or only partially asserted.

Enhancing Public Awareness

And finally, schooling in practical moral reasoning can help pastoral psychotherapists, the institutions for which they work, and the larger church as well to establish—on critical and public grounds—the value commitments that guide their work. It helps to make these commitments appear less arbitrary; historic traditions can be seen to function as hypotheses—accepted in faith—that should be subject to continuing philosophical review and public articulation. It helps to show that what is first accepted in faith can also make sense. And it helps to communicate awareness of the fact that, at the more concrete behavioral levels, what the church advocates has indeed gone through the fires of critical reflection.

It is clear that Jeffrey Builder, as a pastoral psychotherapist, is interested in promoting in a step-by-step manner the next-highest feasible level of moral functioning that is possible for Arthur Strand. The pastor feels that for Arthur it is better to relate than not to relate, and it is better to relate in stable relationships than in one-night stands, even if these relationships have a homosexual dimension and are, for the moment, the only ones possible. What is not clear from the information at hand is whether Jeffrey Builder is interested in the next step—that it is better to relate sexually in a covenanted heterosexual relation than in a homosexual relation. One gathers that the counselor's commitment is in this direction, but we do not know with assurance. For in therapy, as in other fields of life, we balance the morally optimal with the concretely possible. A truly heterosexual relation of a covenanted kind may not be possible for Arthur Strand. But even in helping Arthur to develop cohesion within the context of stable homosexual relations Jeffrey Builder is still in a morally defensible position if he finds some public way to define the context of his counseling as truly supportive of the larger value frameworks that an extended process of moral reasoning indicates should mark the public stand of the ecumenical church. In the face of such public accounting, the special strategies of the pastor's counseling will not be construed as undermining the broader commitments and public role of the church.

CHAPTER 8

Diagnosis
and
Decision

Early in chapter 2 I stated that pastoral care is first of all a matter of care for the systems within which people live. In subsequent chapters we have been developing a method for creating and revising such systems and maintaining them at the normative level. Such systemic effort is certainly a major part of the total task of care.

Never to be forgotten, however, are the actual people within those systems, the specific persons who are sometimes troubled, broken, and in pain. They too, as individuals within the system, need care and concern. No ethical, sociological, reformist, or praxis point of view, however proper its concern for the larger systems, and no caring discipline whether religious or secular should ever forget the people within them. This is why pastoral care needs ways of understanding not only the sociosystems themselves, but also the individuals who are influenced by them.

THE FOUR STEPS OF
PRACTICAL THEOLOGICAL ACTION

Giving help to specific persons involves again an exercise in practical theological thinking and acting. Toward the close of chapter 5 in connection with my proposal of a revised correlational method, I suggested that practical theological action goes through four steps: (1) a step of experiencing and initially defining the problem; (2) a step of attention, listening, and understanding; (3) a step of critical analysis and comparison; and (4) a step of decision and strategy. In terms of this four-step sequence, moving through the five levels of practical moral thinking subsequently described in chapter 6 is properly a part of step three. It involves the kind of analysis and comparison that is required in order critically to reestablish the goal of care. I represent the steps of practical action and the levels of moral reason in figure C.

Figure C

**The Four Steps of Practical Action
Related to
The Five Levels of Practical Reason**

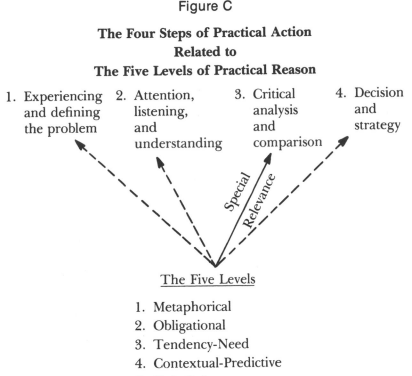

1. Experiencing and defining the problem
2. Attention, listening, and understanding
3. Critical analysis and comparison
4. Decision and strategy

Special Relevance

The Five Levels

1. Metaphorical
2. Obligational
3. Tendency-Need
4. Contextual-Predictive
5. Rule-Role

Fortunately this is not something we have to do each time for each act of care. On most occasions we can rely on the normative capital of the past. But when our traditional goals are called in question or clearly need renovation, we have to start all over again.

It is also possible, however, to apply the same method, the same five levels of practical moral thinking, to a slightly different purpose. Reflective analysis of this kind can help us in our work with individuals. It can help us in our diagnosis or assessment of where individuals are, and how these persons might move toward the goals that are appropriate for them. Hence our discussion turns now to step-three thinking at the point of diagnosis.

THE FIVE LEVELS
AS DIAGNOSTIC GUIDELINES

Until now my presentation of the five levels of practical moral thinking in terms of critical analysis (step three) has treated them as objective categories. They can, however, also be used as subjective categories, as categories of virtue or character—in the language of contemporary moral philosophy, as aretaic categories. We can ask, for example, concerning any particular individual, What are (1) her dominant metaphors of ultimacy; (2) her moral style and patterns; (3) the patterns, modalities, or themes of interaction she uses to meet her needs; (4) the social and cultural forces that shape her context; and (5) the roles and practical rules by which she tries to live her life? The five levels thus give rise to five diagnostic questions that can guide our efforts to understand a particular person. These questions would be used only in due course, at the proper step, only after one had first listened, allowed the person to tell her own story, given her considerable opportunity to set out her problem, restated that problem or issue in the light of further reflection, and in general encouraged the person to communicate her feelings and thoughts. But when the time comes to order all this communication and to analyze it, these five guidelines are proper and useful.

The usefulness of the five levels is enhanced by the fact that they can move in either or both of two directions—toward the normative and toward the descriptive. They can help us answer the question, What *is* the case? And they can help us answer the question, What *should be* the case? The full task of assessment and diagnosis involves answering both questions. The fourth and last step of practical action, the step of decision and strategy, is primarily a matter of finding ways to close the gap between these two levels of diagnosis— the normative and the descriptive. Any act of intervention has as its purpose to find humane, respectful, noncoercive, and nonmoralistic ways to bring these two levels of judgment closer together.

This can happen only if there is flexibility and playfulness in the process of closing the gap between the *is* and the *ought*. Such flexibility and playfulness can emerge because ideally this process is seen as a matter of movement, growth, a pilgrimage, an odyssey. Normally we humans do not and cannot move in one large step, one heroic leap, from where we *are* to where we *ought* to be. Even conversion does not work in this precipitous way; conversions involve a turning, a setting out in a new direction, followed by struggles, by ups and downs, by step-by-step movement. Our goal in care is to hold up—sometimes only by indirection—the next most viable step or goal and to help a person move gradually in that direction, not to impose upon her immediately the highest normative levels and expect their instant attainment.

Furthermore, goal setting—even of the most elementary kind—should be a matter of mutual inquiry between the helper and the person being helped, and never something that one person arbitrarily foists upon the other. In fact, all aspects of arriving at the diagnosis, both descriptive and normative, should be a matter of mutual collaboration and inquiry. Despite this mutuality of inquiry and goal setting, it is still appropriate for the caring agent to become self-conscious and critical with respect to her own methods of making these judgments.

As we seek to specify further the usefulness of the five-level method of practical moral thinking, the following list may prove helpful in guiding our discussion. It suggests the concerns raised at each level when the method is directed to the assessment or diagnosis of persons.

Objective Perspective	Subjective Perspective (Character)
1. Metaphorical	1. Faith Development
2. Obligational	2. Moral Development
3. Tendency-Need	3. Motivational and Emotional Development
4. Contextual-Predictive	4. Ego Development
5. Rule-Role	5. Rule-Role Development

The Faith Level

For purposes of diagnosis we would, at the metaphorical level, be interested primarily in the major metaphors that actually guide a person's life, those which actually constitute her faith with respect to life's realities and possibilities. How do the Christian metaphors of God the creator, God the governor, and God the redeemer actually touch her life?

How does this person feel about God the creator? Does she trust in the goodness of life? Does she trust her own feelings, her own tendencies and needs? Trusting our tendencies and needs does not always mean impulsively acting on them or indulging them but it should mean at the minimum that we can affirm and feel comfortable with all our most pervasive feelings, especially when they are appropriately patterned. Does this person trust the world outside herself? Although the world may not be perfect, does she feel that on the whole people and things outside herself will hold up their end of life's bargains?

How does this person feel about God the governor, about life's need for order, and for limitations on our wants and desires? Does she believe that there is any morality in the nature of things, any objective principles outside herself? Or is life only full of unfairness, partiality, and injustice?

And finally, how does this person feel about God the redeemer? What possibilities does she posit for renewal, change, even redemption? Is life static, closed, unchangeable, and unrenewable? Or is the world experienced as open and full of possibilities for starting again, for being forgiven, for gaining new strength, and for receiving grace?

In *The Minister as Diagnostician* Paul W. Pruyser suggests a variety of theological categories for heuristic use in pastoral assessment. His list is suggestive—which is all he intends for it—but probably one-sided. He mentions such things as awareness of the holy, providence, faith, grace, repentance, communion, and sense of vocation.[1] Pastors can ask where the person in care is with respect to each of these categories: What is her sense of the holy, her sense of God's providence, her awareness of God's grace? Then we can move ahead and contrast these descriptive and empirical judgments about where people actually are with judgments about where they should be as suggested by our normative theological concepts. Most of Pruyser's categories can be organized under one or another of H. Richard Niebuhr's three basic metaphors of God as creator, governor, and redeemer. But, as we shall see in the sections that follow, Pruyser's idea of theological diagnosis can be extended to cover not only the metaphorical level of practical theological thinking, but the four lower levels as well, and especially the obligational level.

It would also be possible, for diagnostic purposes, to use James Fowler's faith-development perspective. Space here does not permit a full elaboration of Fowler's views. Suffice it to say that Fowler regards faith as a certain kind of knowing, a kind of value-knowing or relational-knowing that gives us our sense of basic trust—our sense of the trustworthiness of life and the world. This sense of trust develops in each individual through an invariable sequence of stages. Fowler's "stages of faith development" offer additional help at the metaphorical level in the matter of assessment from the subjective perspective.

The Moral Development Level

For pastoral care there is diagnostic value also at the obligational level. Just as our metaphors of ultimacy influence but never completely dictate our principles of obligation at the level of formal moral decision making, so also our faith influences but does not totally determine our moral development.[2] The faith that we live in a trustworthy world can give us reasons and motivations to be moral, but it does not tell us precisely what being moral means. Yet, as we have seen in our discussion of obligation in chapter 6, being Christian has been associated with the highest principles of impartial love and justice. Hence, assessments about a person's readiness to respond and style of moral responsiveness is a relevant part of pastoral diagnosis. William Frankena suggests that we can even speak about styles of moral character much in the way that we speak about the various formal theories of obligation discussed toward the close of chapter 2.[3] For instance, as we spoke about ethical egoism, we can also speak about trait ethical egoism. Similarly, we can speak about trait act utilitarianism and trait rule utilitarianism, or even about trait act and rule deontology. People who have these character traits would be experienced as having a particular readiness or set to respond to moral situations according to one or more of these several moral perspectives.

The Work of Lawrence Kohlberg

The work of Lawrence Kohlberg can be particularly helpful in making assessments at this aretaic level—which is the characterological counterpart of the obligational level.[4] In fact Kohlberg's work harmonizes well with the position outlined here because his stage six of moral development is strongly influenced by the Kant-Rawls tradition—which, with the help of Ronald Green, I also have used for interpreting the meanings of love and justice. Kohlberg's position is also suggestive because it takes the daring step of claiming that some of the historic options in ethical theory—ethical egoism, utilitarianism, the various deontological positions—can be sorted out as stages of moral development, with some of them naturally coming earlier and some later.

Of course Kohlberg is interested primarily in understanding and measuring one aspect of moral development—our capacity to make moral judgments. He believes, following Jean Piaget, that our capacity to make moral judgments is of a piece with our general capacity to make formal cognitive judgments. In individuals this capacity to make formal cognitive judgments develops over a period of time and follows a certain sequence of maturation and mounting complexity, a pattern of development so universal as to be found in a wide variety of cultures.

In measuring our levels of moral judgment, Kohlberg looks for the way we apply our general cognitive capacities to specified areas of moral discernment. He does this by looking at the reasons people advance for supporting the judgments they make. Kohlberg confronts his subjects with specific moral dilemmas and then asks them in each case for the reasons they would advance to support what they believe is "the right thing to do." The highest stage of ethical judgment, his stage six, is the stage of "universal ethical principles"—the stage that accords with the Kant-Rawls principle of impartial or reversible justice. A person reaches stage six in her moral development when in defense of her judgments she regularly advances reasons having to do with "equality of human rights and respect for the dignity of human beings as individuals."[5] The reader will recall how in my discussion of obligation in chapter 6 I related such principles to the biblical understanding of justice and, by adding active and affective components, to the concept of *agape* as well. Kohlberg's understanding of the highest stage of moral development is clearly of a piece with the theory of obligation I have been proposing.

Kohlberg's Six Stages and Pastoral Assessment

But Kohlberg's work is useful for assessment in pastoral care primarily because his highest stage is placed on a continuum with certain other stages that lead up to it. Let me quickly review Kohlberg's preceding stages of moral development. The first two stages are called preconventional; they occur basically during childhood. Both are egoistic in orientation. In stage one, the punishment and obedience stage, the right thing to do is that which avoids punishment and gains rewards for me. In stage two, the instrumental-hedonist stage, the right thing to do is that which satisfies my interest. The next two stages are more conventional and might be appropriately characterized as primitive deontological stages. In stage three, the interpersonal concordance stage, the right thing to do is that which gains approval from others; here the right thing generally is to conform to the expectations of others. And in stage four, the law and order stage, the right thing to do is that which maintains order in the social system of which one is a part. Stages five and six are postconventional. Stage five, the social contractual stage, is clearly utilitarian: the right thing to do is that which is consistent with what has been democratically agreed upon as producing the greatest good for the social whole. Stage five is distinguishable from the sixth stage because this last and highest stage respects the rights of persons *as persons* even if they stand outside the social contract that binds together a particular group, community, or nation. Hence, stage six is a deontological and universalistic stage which mediates justice to persons as persons.

In pastoral care several interesting uses can be made of Kohlberg's six stages. First, they can be used for purposes of moral diagnosis to discern where a person is in her moral development. They can provide a framework for moral assessment to supplement assessments made at the fifth level discussed a moment ago. Second, and more important, they can provide a way to overcome moralism. This may sound surprising insofar as the six stages are so obviously and exclusively concerned with the moral category. But there is an interesting dimension to Kohlberg's work that is clearly pertinent to the problem of moralism. To induce people to grow morally, Kohlberg tells us, appeals should be made from levels only slightly above their present stage of moral thinking. Stage-two people may be able to understand appeals presented with stage-three reasoning; they probably will not be able to grasp the perspectives of stages five and six. From Kohlberg's perspective, to confront children and adults at lower stages of moral development with unqualified demands may be the height of moralism. This is not to say that we do not want people to grow toward more universalistic moral judgments, but if they are to do this we may need temporarily to bracket the loftier claims and confront the people with claims that are nearer their present level of comprehension and development.

Much of what happens in psychotherapy, whether pastoral or secular, involves precisely this kind of stage approach to growth. The psychiatrist Gene Abroms has pointed out that dynamic insights are used in psychotherapy—and in milder forms of counseling—to mitigate conflict and induce insight, while at the same time the counselor makes subtle appeals from stages of moral reasoning only slightly above where the client is in her own moral thinking.[6] Deepened insight on the part of the client frees her to think and act ethically in slightly more adequate ways. The use of dynamic insight makes it possible for the moral appeals to be more precise, but does not make the psychotherapeutic process any less a moral process.

Something like this is what happened in the case of Arthur Strand. His counselor was seeking primarily to help Arthur experience a more cohesive self and to understand some of his own needs for self-affirmation. Pastor Builder helped Arthur understand that the fulfillment of these needs was a part of his quest for affirmation within the context of a homosexual experience. The pastor's response to Arthur's confession of a transient homosexual experience—"At least you related to someone"—said a great deal. It communicated that the building of relationship was the chief object of Arthur's quest. But it clearly also communicated mild skepticism about the appropriateness of such transient and primitively egoistic relationships, and subtly lifted up slightly more reciprocal and long-lasting possibilities. Thus, within the counseling relationship what was occurring was a subtle moral upgrading, even though the counseling had to do primarily with a restoration of Arthur's basic sense of self-cohesion. An exact transcript of the conversations between Arthur and Jeffrey Builder would probably reveal more precisely—even in terms of Kohlberg's categories—just what kind of upgrading actually occurred.

The Motivational Level

Until now our discussion of the third level of practical moral thinking has been mainly in terms of the central tendencies and needs of persons as members of the human species. Information about these tendencies and needs—which is gained from our intuitive experience, our inherited traditions, and even from the human sciences—is clearly important for moral thinking. Indeed, the just mediation between and organization of these tendencies and needs within the human community can be said to constitute the very stuff of ethical reflection. By making a slight shift in perspective, we can see how these same tendencies and needs constitute also the raw stuff of a person's motivations, emotions, and dynamic behavior. In our discussion of homosexuality we mentioned, for example, our needs for general security or dependence, face-to-face recognition, identity, generativity, and pleasure. One could add many more such human needs—effectance (the need to be a center of causality)[7] and the actualization of certain "higher" potentials[8]—as well as the more basic needs for food, water, and shelter.

But from the perspective of pastoral diagnosis of persons greater interest attaches to the particular styles and modalities of life that an individual uses to satisfy such needs. These styles and modes constitute typical and predictable patterns of interaction with one's interpersonal environment. Some of us humans are more passive than others in handling our needs. Some of us are more actively receptive and positively trusting than others. Some of us are more grasping and acquisitive. Others try to push the world away as if to eliminate an irritating intrusion. Still others of us are intrusive, constantly poking our noses or intruding ourselves generally into other people's lives, business, and privacy.

In addition, our needs and our preferred modes of meeting them can be further qualified by anxiety, guilt, and shame. We can become anxious about loss and threat of loss with respect to our various needs. We can also become guilty and ashamed when other people convince us that our needs and modalities for satisfying them are wrong, bad, or incompetent. Erik Erikson speaks about these various modes for satisfying our central tendencies as "interpersonal modalities,"[9] and an important British school of psychoanalysis speaks of these modes of interpersonal relations as "object relations."[10]

Modalities and Themes

To assess a person psychodynamically is to assess her in terms of the tendencies or needs that motivate her life and the basic modalities and patterns she uses to relate these needs to her interpersonal world. This approach to dynamic psychology is obviously related to the psychoanalytic tradition, but it is most specifically associated with such prominent figures as Erik Erikson, Henry Murray, Robert Lifton, and Kenneth Keniston. It has been used in pastoral psychology by various people and has recently been given powerful and systematic expression by Donald Capps.[11] This tradition of psychology helps us to understand that we all have our preferred modalities for interacting with the world, that at different stages of life we tend to specialize in some modalities more than others, that when our preferred modalities conflict with one another the result can be psychological ambivalence, and that some modalities can become so powerful in our lives as literally to repress other normal and necessary modalities. And finally, these modalities can become elaborated into rather complicated themes which constitute a veritable narrative line to our lives. These themes give a storylike quality to our actions, so that when we are thrust into typical life situations we tend to live out the same themes, become the same story, play the same role, and force others into predictable roles as well.

The various cases to which we have referred in this book can serve to illustrate this idea of modality and theme. Betty Farr, for example, had a strong need for face-to-face affirmation left over from early and deep blows to her narcissistic self-esteem. But she handled this need with certain typical modalities of interaction: she tried to serve and please people—in rather rigid and overdetermined ways.

Jim Farr had a similar need for self-affirmation, but his was built on different dynamic grounds. When his once-powerful father was revealed as weak, Jim as a small boy felt weak and vulnerable as well. But rather than developing a modality of compensation through serving others, he created a modality of compensation through careerism and wealth.

The differing needs and modalities of Jim and Betty Farr produced an unequal and unreciprocal marriage. Although on the face of it Jim had most of the privilege and power, at a deeper level neither Jim nor Betty was able to meet justly the needs of the other. Their psychological conflicts produced an unjust and self-defeating marriage. Their problems were psychological as regards their capacity to act freely and without conflict; their problems were moral from the perspective of the conflicting rights and needs that were being destroyed in the relationship. The ministry and interventions of Peter Spicer, his church, and other helping agencies will need to address the problem of the Farrs at both the dynamic and moral levels in order to be lastingly effective.

Arthur Strand's preferred modality and life theme were quite different. His self-esteem was so connected to merger with his mother that he was afraid that any direct expression of feelings whatsoever, especially with another woman, would lead to the destruction of the other person and, eventually, himself as well. Hence, Arthur's preferred modality was emotional inconspicuousness. It seemed to leave him only one way to handle his sexuality—through transient and drunken homosexual encounters.

Values and Psychodynamic Thinking

Dynamic psychological thinking specializes in understanding and explaining the causal origins of this one line of development which I have called the motivational or emotional line. It tries to (1) identify and understand empathically these modalities and themes, (2) understand which basic human tendencies and needs are being served by them, and (3) explain the developmental and causal origins of these modalities and themes. And finally, dynamic psychological thinking, insofar as it takes place within a caring, helping, or therapeutic relationship, tries to determine ways to influence these needs and modalities toward greater freedom and larger capacity for effective reflection and action. But since free and competent action is always in the service of specific moral and nonmoral values, no caring relationship, no matter how psychodynamically oriented, can ever be strictly neutral about the values which this heightened freedom will eventually serve.

Psychodynamic thinking is primarily retrospective in nature. It tries to identify the patterns, modalities, and themes that function—have functioned and are still functioning—in a person's life. It combines understanding judgments (*Verstehen*) with causal and explanatory judgments about the factors which brought about the modalities it is attempting to understand. But insofar as it gets prospective, thinks about the future, tries to help someone toward health, wholeness, or some optimal condition, however defined, psychodynamic thinking must necessarily become normative and prescriptive—however subtly, gently, artistically, or indirectly this may occur. Insofar as psychodynamic thinking becomes future-oriented, prospective, it is no longer solely psychodynamic; it has to that degree become mixed with other modes of thinking, and in effect become a variation of the kind of practical moral thinking described in this book.

Psychodynamic thinking can be relatively neutral and scientific when it is being prospective—if by prospective one means nothing more than predictive, that is, making estimates about how past modalities are likely to continue in the future. But any judgments about changing or influencing past modalities automatically implicate the helping person in normative judgments of the kind we have been discussing. And insofar as any helper becomes a practical moral thinker, she must go beyond the psychodynamic line of thinking and consider at least some of the other levels of moral thinking as well. Every helper, whether secular or religious, is necessarily at the same time a moral philosopher. Not necessarily a Christian moralist, but if the relation between the metaphorical and obligational levels is as I have claimed in this book, then every helper, whether religious or secular, is inevitably also a religiously oriented moral philosopher.

The Dual Focus of Modalities

Two more important issues need to be discussed in this section on assessment with respect to the motivational line of development. First, there is the question of the relation of the motivational line to the faith line of development. Are not those two really the same thing? Is not the faith line of development really just an aspect of our motivational patterns—our preferred modalities and themes for relating to the world? And finally, since psychology can help us to understand our preferred modalities and themes, can it not also help us to understand our faith at the metaphorical level? In fact, could it be that our faith is nothing more than a projection of the preferred psychosocial modalities and themes that are operative in our lives?

I would answer these questions as follows: Yes, there is a close relationship between our faith and our modalities of social interaction. Yes, psychology can, from a certain perspective, help us understand our faith and our customary metaphors for expressing it. But no, our faiths are not just simple projections of our psychological needs and the habitual modalities we use to meet them.

In fact, our modalities and life themes must be looked at from two angles of vision. They must be looked at from the perspective of the psychological tendencies and needs they are trying to meet. But they must also be viewed from the perspective of what they say about how the world—both social and natural—has actually responded to these tendencies and needs. A modality includes both a self-polarity and a world-polarity; it tells us something about the needs we bring to the world, and it tells us how we have experienced the world responding to our needs. We choose our modalities and keep them because we have come to expect that the way in which the world *seems to have responded in the past* is indicative of the way it is likely to respond in the future. Hence, a modality tells us not only something about our tendencies and needs but also something about the world and the way we have experienced it. And in telling us about such experience it tells us whether we have experienced the world as trustworthy or untrustworthy, good or bad, predictable or capricious, forgiving or moralistic and punitive. Hence, implicit in our modalities of interaction is our faith about the kind of world we live in, our faith about *how the world seems to be.*

Hence, modalities and themes are not just a projection of our tendencies, wishes, and needs. A modality is not just a creation of our imagination. It contains a statement, a belief; it expresses our faith about how the world actually is. This faith is based on the way we have experienced at least certain portions of the world in the past. Hence, buried in every modality and life theme is something of an ontological affirmation about how the world is or *seems to be* at its very core or essence.

There is little doubt that if we have experienced our mothers and fathers as bad—vindictive, ungenerous, unempathic, capricious— we are likely to feel that this is the way the world is at its very depth. We are likely even to think that this is the way God is. Our mother and father, and other early figures who mediate to us our first experience of the world and its possibilities become symbolic and representative—metaphors—of the whole. But the basic presupposition of all help and counseling, whether secular or religious, is that the way we have experienced the world in the past—possibly when we were quite young—does not exhaust the final meaning of the world and its possibilities. Mother may have been bad, even rotten, but all mothers are not like her. There is something in human nature—something behind and above it too—that makes most mothers pretty decent sorts. The same is true of fathers, and of brothers and sisters, leaders, people in general, and even God. Every change agent, every pastor, pastoral counselor, pastoral psychotherapist, and even every secular counselor believes that the past ways in which the world has hurt us do not exhaust its final possibilities. They all believe that there are grounds for a different set of expectations, grounds for altering our preferred modalities and themes in such a way that we become open to possibilities to which we were once quite blind. And they all try in their several ways to mediate a different view of the world's possibilities to the people they seek to help. Hence, a psychodynamic perspective, while it can help us to understand better the modalities and themes of our life, does not thereby reduce these themes to simple projections of our psychological tendencies and needs.

Moral and Motivational Levels in Pastoral Assessment

And finally, I want to add a word about the relation of the motivational to the moral developmental lines of assessment. Although the two clearly overlap and interpenetrate, they are nonetheless distinguishable. Our cognitive capacities to make reversible judgments are certainly conditioned by our emotional and motivational patterns. If emotionally we are highly dependent, for example, it will be difficult for us to move beyond a conventional level of moral judgment. People who have been prematurely cast out by parental figures, forced into precocious independence, or angered through subtle rejection often have emotional needs that make it difficult for them to go beyond an instrumental-hedonistic stage of moral development. In short, one's character is influenced by both the faith above it and the motivational patterns below it. People who do not trust the world in some general way rarely feel that being moral is worthwhile. And, as I have just pointed out, if our preferred modalities of interaction are passive, or grasping, or tight and retentive, this is likely to affect the style of our moral judgments as well.

Sometimes in our pastoral assessment, we confuse the moral and motivational levels. In his excellent *Pastoral Care: A Thematic Approach* Capps does this in one of his case studies.[12] Here he tells an engaging story about a young couple who suddenly decide to get married when Valerie's parents begin objecting to her visits to Bill's apartment. The minister who begins to discuss with them their impending marriage hears their forceful claim that they have thought about their decision carefully and worked out all the problems, but it quickly becomes apparent that they have not. A male friend with whom Bill has shared his apartment will continue to live with them, they say, though they have not agreed on how to share the rent or how to divide the housekeeping chores; nor have they reached an agreement about whether Bill will be faithful to Valerie and stop flirting with other women. In commenting on this case

Capps says that the pastoral interview uncovered "the theme of mutual rights." This is true, but Capps offers this case in the first place as an example of his theory of psychological themes. Mutual rights is not a psychological theme in the same sense as dependence, or martyrdom, or anxious acquisitiveness, or others one might name. Mutual rights is rather a moral issue about the question of just rights and obligations within the marriage relationship. The psychodynamic question is, What are the modalities and personality themes in Bill and Valerie that make them blind to these moral issues? Capps's assessment affords a beautiful instance of how moral issues actually surface in and come to the focus of our care even when we are unaware of them or call them by different names.

Ego Development and the Contextual Level

Of the next two levels in personal diagnosis we can speak more briefly. In making assessments at the fourth level, we should avoid clear-cut choices between the objective and subjective points of view. While we want to know objectively as much as possible about the person's context, both social and cultural, we want also to know how realistic she is in her perception of that context.

The capacity for realistic judgment about the dimensions of one's personal and social context is often thought to be a matter of ego capacity—the central perceptual and organizing capacities of the human organism. In helping people, we always want to have some sense of how they actually perceive their circumstances and what is in fact their general capacity for making realistic judgments.

In speaking about this matter of reality testing as a distinct developmental capacity, I am not suggesting that it is totally unrelated to other developmental lines such as the capacity for moral judgments or our preferred psychosocial modalities and themes. These capacities too make use of certain perceptual capacities of the ego. But by introducing the idea of the reality-testing capacity of the ego, I am simply suggesting another perspective from which to view people and relating this fourth level to a huge body of literature in the field called ego psychology, thereby helping the reader to fit such material into the frameworks offered in this book.

Rule and Role Development

The level of rules and roles is a highly complex and highly concrete level of development. In fact, it is so complex precisely because it is so concrete. We arrive at our practical rules and everyday roles only after we make conscious or unconscious judgments at all the other levels.

In making assessments at this level we ask questions such as these: Does the person know what roles she is being asked to play in various situations? Does she understand the implicit or explicit rules that govern these roles? Does she affirm these rules or fight against them? Does the person have any role distance, any capacity to think critically about roles? Can she gain any objectivity about or perspective on the roles and expectations within which she finds herself? And finally, does the person have the capacity to be innovative? Can she change roles, or change the rules and expectations connected with her roles—and do so fairly, justly, trustingly? Can the person relate her roles to the other four levels of practical moral thinking? This last question about a person's capacity to change roles in reality raises the entire question of practical moral thinking.

But the level of rules and roles is also the level of practical strategy and implementation. It is the level where we must decide what actually should be done and *how* to do it. For this reason I will at this point stop our discussion of pastoral diagnosis and assessment, and turn directly to the question of strategies of implementation. Such discussion could in itself warrant a whole book. The discussion here is designed only to be suggestive. A fuller treatment must await a later occasion.

THE FOURTH STEP:
DECISION AND STRATEGY

Diagnosis is important in any caring situation because it helps us decide what to do. The reader, however, despite our extensive discussion of assessment, should be warned against taking a technicist or hyperanalytic attitude toward helping anyone. The rubrics I have here suggested are intended only as heuristic guidelines, something to keep in the back of the mind to guide inquiry and reflection. They can seldom be applied with elegance—we almost never have enough information. They can serve as little more than checkpoints to help us review and order our reflection.

Discerning the Primary Issue

The same caution is to be observed as regards the way these guidelines can assist us in deciding *how* to care for other people. Sometimes our care addresses primarily the metaphorical and faith levels of a person's life. Sometimes it focuses primarily on the obligational and moral-development levels. Sometimes it focuses on the need, motivational, and modality patterns. Sometimes our help is quite expedient and tries primarily to alleviate the distressing pressures—poverty, discrimination, illness—that come from a person's social and cultural context. Sometimes our help addresses the concrete level of the governing roles and rules.

Frequently our care addresses all of these levels. Often the question of strategy then becomes one of deciding which is the primary issue, and what we—because of our social role and skills—are best able to address. It should be obvious that there is no way to address any human problem without sooner or later touching all of these levels of practical moral thinking and action. The task of pastoral care is to show a readiness to deal with all of them—which is what we mean when we speak of dealing with "the whole person." But even the pastor who is prepared and ready to address all levels may conclude that under certain circumstances only one or two of them are the most important and constitute the strategic point where leverage must be greatest if the care is to be truly caring and of maximum help to that person.

Psychological Problems and Faith Problems

For instance, in almost all of the cases discussed in this book, the levels most in need of primary concern and attention were (1) the metaphorical and faith level, and (2) the tendency-need and motivational level. We may recall these cases from the perspective of these two concerns.

Jim and Betty Farr are not going to be able to address the question of just and reciprocal relations in their marriage, important as these are, until they develop more flexible modalities of relating to each other. Whether their problem is a matter of faith or a matter of psychological modality is strictly a question of which angle of vision one uses to think about the issue. Jim and Betty both have deep problems with their feelings of worthlessness and self-depreciation. Both of them feel, for important but different reasons, that they are not much good—and that the world in which they live is not very trustworthy, responsive, or reciprocal. Looked at retrospectively, the problem might appear psychological because their modalities of life derive initially from their experiences of early childhood, their relationships with their parents. But looked at prospectively, the problem is a matter of faith. Jim and Betty need new ways of discerning the possibilities of the world—its potential trustworthiness, responsiveness, and nurturance. They need new metaphors for reading the world.

If Peter Spicer, his congregation, and whatever professional help he gets for the Farrs can all offer new possibilities of relating—new acceptance, new prizing, new consistency of recognition, new love—they may succeed in helping the couple see and feel the world in new and different ways. Potentially, all of these relationships constitute for the Farrs new prisms through which to see the world. Minister, church members, and therapist all offer their own persons as metaphors of the more general possibilities latent in the world. Somewhere in all these relationships, metaphors about the goodness of creation and the redemptive possibilities within it will be implicitly or explicitly present.

Although this attention to faith and the metaphors of ultimacy would need to be the primary focus, it should not be the sole focus of care with Jim and Betty Farr. In ways which Pastor Spicer originally underestimated, their moral responsibility to one another, pledged in their marriage covenant, needs also to be upheld. A gentle but deep valuing of these self-transcending and *agapic* marriage promises needs to be communicated—an appropriate role for Pastor Spicer. Much of what he is doing for this couple moves in the right direction; some of his interpretation of what he is doing, however, is faulty. The metaphor of God as governor confronts us with a diffuse but real obligational dimension of Christianity. The new strength that we hope the Farrs will someday acquire should be used finally to enhance *agapic* fidelity to one another, their children, and other people. And even if for the Farrs that outcome should finally prove impossible in their concrete relations with each other, such love and justice should nonetheless remain the general goal of their lives. The obligational level should be in the background of all our care for the Farrs, even though it may not be the appropriate first point of entry.

One additional word is in order about Pastor Spicer's referral of the Farrs to a professional psychotherapist. Was that a good thing to do? In this case it probably was. But why? Well, not because their problems are uniquely or entirely psychological. As we have said, whether the problem is regarded as psychological or a matter of faith is strictly a question of whether one takes the retrospective or the prospective point of view. A professional therapist, whether pastoral or secular, can perhaps be more precise in mediating the deep and consistent sense of personal presence that Jim and Betty both need. The professional may have the time, the structure, and the diagnostic skills needed to understand and better address the needs, modalities, and themes that are ruling their lives. But when it comes time to offer through the therapeutic relationship a new view of the world—a new faith—the therapist will logically be no different from the pastor and the members of his congregation. And more often than not, even for allegedly secular therapists, the world to which the therapeutic relation bears witness will be at best vaguely reminiscent of major themes celebrated explicitly by the Judeo-Christian tradition.[13]

Ethical Confrontation

The prominence of the metaphorical and motivational levels may be less pronounced in the case of Bill and Valerie. We do not know—or at least the pastor makes no report—about any deep-seated preoedipal problems with either of them. Let us assume that their childhoods were stronger, and that Bill and Valerie accordingly have a stronger sense of self than do either of the Farrs. Addressing the question of just and fair relationships in marriage may well be more appropriate for them. If done in a gentle and affirming way, it might be just the thing to help mitigate their rambunctious and impulsive youthfulness. In fact, it is clear that in the course of his interview, as Capps reports it, the minister skillfully initiated just this kind of moral inquiry into the relation between Bill and Valerie, an inquiry that, until then, they had largely avoided themselves.

For a person with a relatively well-differentiated personality, a reasonably strong sense of self, a fairly intact superego, and a reasonably adequate perceptual or ego capacity, direct moral confrontation can often be valuable, especially in the case of people who clearly have had the freedom more or less self-consciously to misuse these strengths. These are the kinds of cases that authors such as Hobart Mowrer, William Glasser, and their pastoral followers have in mind. And this is a point beautifully made and well illustrated in John Hoffman's Ethical Confrontation in Counseling.[14] People who can profit from ethical confrontation are those who have enough ego and superego actually to feel guilt. Often such people need to have this guilt named. Frequently they need to experience rituals of forgiveness and restoration before they can feel whole once again.

Such confrontation and ritual have been traditional tasks of pastors throughout the ages.

But it would be a mistake to assume that this is what everyone needs or, at least, needs first and foremost. All of us have failed, all of us have sinned, and all of us have misused our freedom. All of us need rituals of restoration *sooner or later*. But for individuals such as Jim and Betty Farr and Arthur Strand, this is not the first order of business; it may come later. For people such as Bill and Valerie it might appropriately come a little sooner.

The point of talking about the moral context of pastoral care or about the relation of psychological and moral judgments is not exhausted by the narrower question of the role of moral confrontation in care and counseling. The purposes of the larger discussion have to do with how we maintain a moral universe, ground it within the context of a pluralistic world, and still have the flexibility to set parts of it aside temporarily in certain moments of care or use it nonarbitrarily in other moments when it is relevant.

CHAPTER 9

The Church as Community of Moral Discourse

Unfortunately this book—as is generally the case with books on pastoral care—has concentrated too much on individuals, though we have compensated for this somewhat by discussing how to think normatively about the systems within which individuals invariably stand. Furthermore, we have spoken mainly about one-to-one relationships, often with primary focus on the minister as helping agent. And finally, except in the case of Arthur Strand (and possibly the Farrs), we have spoken generally about care within the context of the congregation, without discussing sufficiently the question of care in the public world outside the congregation.

But with a little imagination, what has been said about practical moral thinking, about diagnosis and strategies of intervention, can be applied equally well to the ministry of the congregation as a whole. In fact, our five levels can be used to guide a congregation in its practical moral inquiry and care.

A friend of mine serving a suburban church has used something like these five levels of practical moral inquiry to order the pastoral care of his congregation. Sometimes this church uses the five levels to address issues of care outside the congregation. The minister has a pastoral care group that regularly asks itself certain questions when discussing an issue in care.

After identifying in a preliminary way what the problem is, they ask, What theological images or symbols can help us further define and address this problem? The question is obviously couched at the metaphorical level of practical moral thinking. The people discuss the question informally. Wide participation is encouraged. People are asked to exercise imagination, think creatively, and speak with spontaneous and unguarded freedom. More careful theological, philosophical, and biblical work can come later.

Then they are asked, What human needs does this problem entail? This question is obviously close to our level three—the tendency-need level. It is also a further extension of the effort to understand and define the problem.

But then the people return to what sounds like level two. They ask, What have we done about this problem in the past and what should we do now? This clearly brings up the obligational level of moral thinking. Once again, they are asked first to speculate freely and suggest spontaneously before taking steps in the direction of more careful theological and biblical work.

Their fourth question is this, What can we do about this problem? Here the question clearly gets into the contextual-predictive dimensions of moral thinking. It invites the group to think about the possibilities of and limits to their actions. In this connection sociological and cultural analysis, formal or informal, would be helpful. If applied rigorously, the question would ask what needs can be justly actualized *by us*—by this group, this church, now in our situation—in the light of realistic social, psychological, and cultural constraints.

And finally, they ask, What should our concrete strategy be? This question voices a concern similar to our concern with the concrete roles and rules that guide specific strategies of action. This gets to the practicalities and ethics of assigning tasks, being responsible, determining procedures, following routines, and developing consistent and dependable patterns of action that will get things done.

Inherent in these five simple and straightforward questions is the whole task of practical moral thinking as applied to the task of care. Of course, the questions can be answered with varying degrees of rigor. They can be answered following a logic different from that outlined in chapter 6. The metaphors, the theories of obligation, the understanding of needs, contexts, and rules and roles may be relatively adequate or inadequate, Christian or non-Christian, truly caring or basically destructive. To the extent that this group, or any other group, uses questions such as these to guide their care, they are doing essentially what I have been talking about in this book.

These questions and the procedures they imply can be used to address any moral question the church may be facing, including any question of care. They apply whether the church is dealing with the sick or with the problem of alcoholism and drug abuse, whether it is confronting problems of sexuality and marriage or the unique stresses and strains found in particular communities or neighborhoods. They can be used to address problems of death and dying or the depression and hopelessness of a parish area marked by chronic unemployment. All the problems mentioned in the first chapter of this book—teenage sexuality, suicide, delinquency—can be approached by way of these questions and the method of practical moral thinking that they imply and employ.

All problems of care are finally, in some way, moral problems—in the full and nonformalist meaning of "morality" as I have used the term in this book. It is only when everyone seems to agree about *how* to be truly helpful that we sometimes overlook the moral status of the particular issues we may be facing. This kind of agreement is increasingly rare in today's world.

As I conclude this book I am trying to imagine what may be in the minds of my readers. I can picture many of you asking, Is caring for another all this complicated? The answer, of course, is that it is not—especially if we *know* what to do. And much of the time, we do know, or at least we think we know. Most of the time we simply draw upon the traditional fund of procedures, goals, and values of care that have been delivered to us. And most of the time these traditions, both religious and secular, are trustworthy. We get our start by becoming sensitive to these great traditions and imitating them. But we live in a society full of innovation and pluralism. So we sometimes fuss over the most trivial matters in our caring for others—trivial, that is, unless we understand that beneath the seemingly trivial differences there are sometimes completely different metaphorical understandings of what is ultimate, different theories of obligation, and different understandings of what humans really want or need or deserve to have. When this shock of recognition occurs, we must at least for a moment give up our illusions of life's simplicity, and begin to think in fresh ways, even with regard to such elementary tasks as how to show love for our neighbor. The methodologies discussed in this book are designed to contribute to this unwanted but inevitable task.

Notes

1. Pluralism, Modernity, and Care

1. Talcott Parsons, *Social Structure and Personality* (New York: Free Press of Glencoe, 1964).

2. Peter Berger, *The Sacred Canopy* (Garden City, N.Y.: Doubleday & Co., 1967), 17, 141–71.

2. The Estrangement of Care from Ethics

1. E. Mansell Pattison, *Pastor and Parish—A Systems Approach*, ed. Howard J. Clinebell and Howard J. Stone (Philadelphia: Fortress Press, 1977).

2. Robert Bonthius, "Pastoral Care for Structures as Well as Persons," *Pastoral Psychology* 18 (May 1967):10–19.

3. Don S. Browning, *The Moral Context of Pastoral Care* (Philadelphia: Westminster Press, 1976).

4. Heinz Kohut, *The Analysis of the Self: A Systematic Approach to the Psychoanalytic Treatment of Narcissistic Personality Disorders* (New York: International Universities Press, 1971).

5. Ibid., 7–11.

6. William Frankena, *Ethics*, 2d ed. (Englewood Cliffs, N.J.: Prentice-Hall, 1973), 14.

7. Ibid., 17.

8. Ibid., 15.

9. Joseph Fletcher, *Situation Ethics: The New Morality* (Philadelphia: Westminster Press, 1966).

10. John Giles Milhaven, *Toward a New Catholic Morality* (Garden City, N.Y.: Doubleday & Co., 1970).

3. The Movement Toward Ethical Neutrality

1. See, for example, Stanley Hauerwas, *Vision and Virtue: Essays in Christian Ethical Reflection* (Notre Dame, Ind.: Fides/Claretian, 1974), 11–29.

2. Reinhold Niebuhr, *The Nature and Destiny of Man: A Christian Interpretation* (New York: Charles Scribner's Sons, 1941), 151–52.

3. For the relation of psychology and ethics in William James see Don S. Browning, *Pluralism and Personality: William James and Some Contemporary Cultures of Psychology* (East Brunswick, N.J.: Bucknell University Press, 1980), 211–36.

4. Sigmund Freud, "Project for a Scientific Psychology," in *The Origins of Psycho-Analysis: Letters to Wilhelm Fliess, Drafts and Notes, 1872–1902,* ed. M. Bonaparte et al. (New York: Basic Books, 1954).

5. Erik Erikson, *Insight and Responsibility* (New York: W. W. Norton, 1964), 17–46.

6. Heinz Hartmann, *Psychoanalysis and Moral Values* (New York: International Universities Press, 1960), 20–21.

7. Carl Rogers, *Client-Centered Therapy: Its Current Practice, Implications and Theory* (Boston: Houghton Mifflin, 1951), 487–92; Abraham H. Maslow, *Toward a Psychology of Being* (Princeton, N.J.: D. Van Nostrand, 1962), 146–51.

8. Frankena, *Ethics*, 15.

9. David Norton, *Personal Destinies: A Philosophy of Ethical Individualism* (Princeton, N.J.: Princeton University Press, 1976), 3–41.

10. Erich Fromm, *Man for Himself: An Inquiry Into the Psychology of Ethics* (New York: Rinehart & Co., 1947), 18–30.

11. Sigmund Freud, *The Problem of Anxiety,* Eng. trans. H. A. Bunker (New York: W. W. Norton, 1936).

12. Sigmund Freud, *Civilization and Its Discontents,* Eng. trans. and ed. J. Strachey (New York: W. W. Norton, 1962).

13. Carl Rogers, "A Theory of Therapy, Personality, and Interpersonal Relationships," in *Psychology: A Study of a Science,* ed. Sigmund Koch, 7 vols. (New York: McGraw-Hill, 1959), 3:23–24.

14. Carl Rogers, *On Becoming a Person* (Boston: Houghton Mifflin, 1961), 118.

15. Seward Hiltner, *Pastoral Counseling* (Nashville: Abingdon-Cokesbury Press, 1949), 49–51.

16. Ibid., 97.

17. Ibid., 148.

18. Seward Hiltner, *Preface to Pastoral Theology* (Nashville: Abingdon Press, 1958), 20–29, 148.

19. Ibid., 149–50.

20. Ibid., 151.

21. Howard Clinebell, *Basic Types of Pastoral Counseling* (Nashville: Abingdon Press, 1966), 27–56.

22. Ibid., 227.

23. Ibid., 225.

4. Trends in Protestant and Catholic Ethics

1. Stephen Toulmin, *Human Understanding*, vol. 1, *Concepts: Their Collective Use and Evolution* (Princeton, N.J.: Princeton University Press, 1972), 359–411.

2. James Gustafson, *Protestant and Roman Catholic Ethics: Prospects for Rapprochement* (Chicago: University of Chicago Press, 1978), 2–3.

3. Thomas C. Oden, *The Intensive Group Experience: The New Pietism* (Philadelphia: Westminster Press, 1972).

4. John Calvin, *Institutes of the Christian Religion*, Eng. trans. J. T. McNeill, 2 vols. (Philadelphia: Westminster Press, 1960), 367–68.

5. Gustafson, *Protestant and Roman Catholic Ethics*, 19.

5. Method in Practical Moral Thinking

1. James Gustafson, *The Church as Moral Decision-Maker* (New York: United Church Press, 1970).

2. Avery Dulles, *Models of the Church* (Dublin: Gill & MacMillan, 1976), 75–80.

3. Richard E. Palmer, *Hermeneutics: Interpretation Theory in Schleiermacher, Dilthey, Heidegger, and Gadamer* (Evanston, Ill.: Northwestern University Press, 1969), 14.

4. Hans-Georg Gadamer, *Truth and Method* (New York: Seabury Press, 1975).

5. David Tracy, *The Analogical Imagination: Christian Theology and the Culture of Pluralism* (New York: Crossroad, 1981), 154–92.

6. Richard Rorty, *Philosophy and the Mirror of Nature* (Princeton, N.J.: Princeton University Press, 1979), 318.

7. For excellent discussions of the relation of theory to practice, see Richard Bernstein, *Praxis and Action: Contemporary Philosophies of Human Activity* (Philadelphia: University of Pennsylvania Press, 1971), ix–xv, and Thomas Groome, *Christian Religious Education: Sharing Our Story and Vision* (New York: Harper & Row, 1980), 152–83.

8. Groome, *Christian Religious Education*, 184–206.

9. David Tracy, *Blessed Rage for Order: The New Pluralism in Theology* (New York: Seabury Press, 1975), 32–63; idem, *Analogical Imagination*.

10. James D. Whitehead and Evelyn E. Whitehead, *Method in Ministry: Theological Reflection and Christian Ministry* (New York: Seabury Press, 1980), 2, 12–19.

11. Ibid., 21–25.

12. Tracy, *Blessed Rage for Order*, 64–87.

6. The Five Levels of Practical Moral Thinking

1. Paul Ricoeur, "The Hermeneutics of Symbols and Philosophical Reflection," *International Philosophical Quarterly* 2 (1962):191–218.

2. George Lakoff and Mark Johnson, *Metaphors We Live By* (Chicago: University of Chicago Press, 1980), 5.

3. H. Richard Niebuhr, *The Responsible Self* (New York: Harper & Row, 1963).

4. Norton, *Personal Destinies*, 40, 306–9.

5. See James Gustafson's Introduction to H. R. Niebuhr, *Responsible Self*, 30.

6. See especially Ernest Wallwork's discussion, "Morality, Religion, and Kohlberg's Theory," in *Moral Development, Moral Education, and Kohlberg*, ed. Brenda Munsey (Birmingham, Ala.: Religious Education Press, 1980), 214–31.

7. Hauerwas, *Vision and Virtue*, 71.

8. Ibid., 73.

9. William James, *The Meaning of Truth: A Sequel to Pragmatism* (Ann Arbor: University of Michigan Press, 1970), 227.

10. James M. Gustafson, *Christ and the Moral Life* (Chicago: University of Chicago Press, 1976), 34.

11. John Rawls, *A Theory of Justice* (Cambridge: Harvard University Press, 1971), 11–22.

12. Ronald Green, *Religious Reason: The Rational and Moral Basis of Religious Belief* (New York and Oxford: Oxford University Press, 1978).

13. Ibid., 159–62.

14. Ibid., 1.

15. Ibid., 130.

16. Ibid., 132.

17. Mary Midgley, *Beast and Man: The Roots of Human Nature* (Ithaca, N.Y.: Cornell University Press, 1978).

18. George Pugh, *The Biological Origin of Human Values* (New York: Basic Books, 1977).

19. Peter Singer, *The Expanding Circle: Ethics and Sociobiology* (New York: Farrar, Straus & Giroux, 1981).

7. Two Case Studies

1. See my discussion of how developmental resolutions become a guide to generative love in *The Generative Man: Psychological Perspectives* (Philadelphia: Westminster Press, 1973), 179–97; see also Kohut, *Analysis of the Self*, 300–308.

2. Don Evans, *Faith, Authenticity, and Morality* (Toronto: University of Toronto Press, 1980), 3–10.

3. Thomas C. Oden, *Kerygma and Counseling* (Philadelphia: Westminster Press, 1966); Don S. Browning, *Atonement and Psychotherapy* (Philadelphia: Westminster Press, 1966); Tracy, *Blessed Rage for Order*, 91–119; Stephen Toulmin, *The Place of Reason in Ethics* (Cambridge: Cambridge University Press, 1970), 202–14.

4. Don S. Browning, "Homosexuality, Theology, the Social Sciences and the Church," *Encounter* 40 (Summer 1979):223–43.

5. "A Study Document on Homosexuality and the Church," Resolution No. 7750, *Empowered by Love*, General Assembly of the Christian Church (Disciples of Christ), (October 1977):191–201.

6. *Human Sexuality: A Preliminary Study* (New York: United Church Press, 1977).

7. *Blue Book I, The Church and the Homosexual*, The General Assembly of the United Presbyterian Church, 1978.

8. *Human Sexuality*, 76.

9. "A Study Document on Homosexuality," 192.

10. *Human Sexuality*, 85.

11. *The Church and the Homosexual*, 163.

12. Ibid., 167.

13. "A Study Document on Homosexuality," 197; *Human Sexuality*, 139.

14. William H. Masters and Virginia E. Johnson, *Homosexuality in Perspective* (Boston: Little, Brown & Co., 1979), 411.

15. *Human Sexuality*, 187.

16. Ibid., 188–91.

17. "A Study Document on Homosexuality," 193–94.

18. *The Church and the Homosexual*, 167.

19. Ibid., 187–88.

20. Ibid.

21. Helmut Thielicke, *The Ethics of Sex* (New York: Harper & Row, 1964).

22. Judd Marmor, ed., *Sexual Inversion* (New York: Basic Books, 1965), 113–14.

23. Erikson, *Insight and Responsibility*, 130.

24. Ibid., 131–32.

25. Marvin K. Opler, "Anthropological and Cross-Cultural Aspects of Homosexuality," in *Sexual Inversion*, ed. Marmor, 111.

8. Diagnosis and Decision

1. Paul W. Pruyser, *The Minister As Diagnostician: Personal Problems in Pastoral Perspective* (Philadelphia: Westminster Press, 1976), 61–79.

2. Wallwork, "Morality, Religion, and Kohlberg's Theory."

3. Frankena, *Ethics*, 63–65.

4. Lawrence Kohlberg, *The Philosophy of Moral Development: Essays in Moral Development*, vol. 1 (New York: Harper & Row, 1981).

5. Ibid., 412.

6. Gene Abroms, "The Place of Values in Psychotherapy," *Journal of Marriage and Family Counseling* (October 1978):3–17.

7. Robert White, *Ego and Reality in Psychoanalytic Theory* (New York: International Universities Press, 1963), 33–37.

8. Abraham H. Maslow, *Motivation and Personality* (New York: Harper &

Brothers, 1954), 146–54.

9. Erik Erikson, *Childhood and Society*, rev. ed. (New York: W. W. Norton, 1964), 44–92.

10. Harry Guntrip, *Psychoanalytic Theory, Therapy, and the Self* (New York: Basic Books, 1971), 90.

11. Donald Capps, *Pastoral Care: A Thematic Approach* (Philadelphia: Westminster Press, 1979), 19–30.

12. Ibid., 98–107.

13. See Oden, *Kerygma and Counseling*, and Browning, *Atonement and Psychotherapy*.

14. John Hoffman, *Ethical Confrontation in Counseling* (Chicago: University of Chicago Press, 1979).